PHILIP ALLAN
LITERATURE GUIDE
FOR GCSE

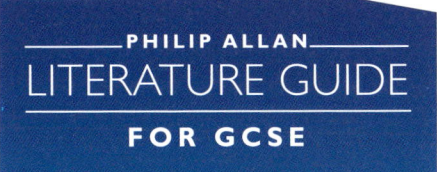

ROMEO AND JULIET
WILLIAM SHAKESPEARE

Robert Francis

With thanks to Jeanette Weatherall for reviewing the manuscript of this book

Philip Allan Updates, an imprint of Hodder Education, an Hachette UK company, Market Place, Deddington, Oxfordshire OX15 0SE

Orders

Bookpoint Ltd, 130 Milton Park, Abingdon, Oxfordshire OX14 4SB

tel: 01235 827720

fax: 01235 400454

e-mail: uk.orders@bookpoint.co.uk

Lines are open 9.00 a.m.–5.00 p.m., Monday to Saturday, with a 24-hour message answering service. You can also order through the Philip Allan Updates website: www.philipallan.co.uk

© Philip Allan Updates 2010

ISBN 978-1-4441-1025-8

First printed 2010

Impression number 5 4 3 2 1

Year 2015 2014 2013 2012 2011 2010

WEST SUSSEX COUNTY LIBRARY SERVICE	
200981254	
Askews & Holts	22-Nov-2011
822.3 SHA	

All rights reserved; no part of this publication may be reproduced, stored in a retrieval system, or transmitted, in any other form or by any means, electronic, mechanical, photocopying, recording or otherwise without either the prior written permission of Philip Allan Updates or a licence permitting restricted copying in the United Kingdom issued by the Copyright Licensing Agency Ltd, Saffron House, 6–10 Kirby Street, London EC1N 8TS.

Cover photo reproduced by permission of Photostage

Page graphic courtesy of Speculare/Fotolia

Printed in Spain

Hachette UK's policy is to use papers that are natural, renewable and recyclable products and made from wood grown in sustainable forests. The logging and manufacturing processes are expected to conform to the environmental regulations of the country of origin.

Contents

Getting the most from
this book and website 2

Introduction 4

Context 7

Plot and structure 12

Characterisation 32

Style 46

Themes 58

Tackling the assessments 64

Assessment Objectives and skills 76

Sample essays 81

Answers 92

Getting the most from this book and website

You may find it useful to read sections of this guide when you need them, rather than reading it from start to finish. For example, the section on *Context* can be read before you read the play itself. This section offers many clues to how an Elizabethan audience might have reacted to the play and how this might differ from the reactions of a modern audience.

The following features have been used throughout this guide.

Target your thinking

● **What are the play's main themes?**

A list of **introductory questions** to target your thinking is provided at the beginning of each chapter. Look back at these once you have read the chapter and check you have understood each of them before you move on.

Build critical skills

Broaden your thinking about the text by answering the questions in the **Pause for thought** boxes. They are intended to encourage you to consider your own opinions in order to develop your skills of criticism and analysis.

Pause for thought

Grade-boosting advice

Pay particular attention to the **Grade booster** boxes. Students with a firm grasp of these ideas are likely to be aiming for the top grades.

Grade *booster*

PHILIP ALLAN LITERATURE GUIDE **FOR GCSE**

Key quotations are highlighted for you, and you may wish to use these as evidence in your examination answers. Line references are given for the Cambridge School edition of the text (ISBN 978-0-521-61870-0. '1.5 137–38' means Act 1 scene 5 lines 137–38.

Key quotation

'My only love sprung from my only hate!'
(1.5 137–38)

Be exam-ready

The **Grade focus** sections explain how you may be assessed and distinguish between higher and foundation responses.

Grade *focus*

Get the top grades

Use the **Text focus** boxes to practise evaluating the text in detail and looking for evidence to support your understanding.

Text focus

Develop evaluation skills

Review your learning

Test your knowledge

Use the **Review your learning** sections to test your knowledge after you have read each chapter. Answers to the questions are provided in the final section of the guide.

Don't forget to go online for even more free revision activities and self-tests:
www.philipallan.co.uk/literatureguidesonline

Introduction

How to approach the text

A play is, above all, designed to be performed. A large part of the playwright's art is to engage and involve the audience, by making us active participants in assessing the actions and reactions of the characters on the stage to the various events and settings created for them. However, any play consists of much more than its events. You need to know the basic storyline well to gain a good mark in either your exam or Controlled Assessment, but if you simply retell the story, you will not gain a high mark. Your examiner will be assessing how far you are aware of what Shakespeare may be trying to say to us *through* his play. This is known as the subtext.

In order to appreciate Shakespeare's subtext in this play, you need to study his characters carefully. Their actions, their words and their individual characteristics have all been created by Shakespeare quite consciously, to convey his thoughts and ideas about the world in which he lived and the values of that world: Elizabethan England. The setting of the play is also an important factor. It is not purely incidental that the play is set in Italy rather than in England, so we have to address the question of why Shakespeare might have done this (see *Context* for more on this).

As students of *Romeo and Juliet*, your task is made more problematic than with many modern plays, in that there are not many stage directions and this lays the play wide open to interpretation. However, the language of the play itself helps to keep modern producers in check. If we examine exactly what lines of speech the characters have been given by Shakespeare, the possible interpretations of the text are narrowed.

While this guide is no substitute for a careful and thoughtful reading of the play itself, it will give you an insight into possible interpretations of the play and help you to build the confidence needed to reach your own conclusions and express your own views.

How to revise the text

The examiner will be checking to see that you have an understanding of:
- *what* Shakespeare may be saying
- *how* he is saying it
- *how effectively* you think he has said it

Introduction

In your revision, start with the themes of the play (*what* he is saying). From here, it is a logical step to remind yourself of *how* Shakespeare reveals, highlights, emphasises, reinforces or underlines these themes to us through:
- the characters he has created (characterisation)
- the language he gives these characters to speak (style)
- the events he subjects these characters to (plot and structure)
- the timing of these events (plot and structure)
- the reactions he gives his characters to these events and to one another (characterisation)
- his use of symbolism (style)

While you are showing off your knowledge of these techniques, you will also want to give your view of *how effectively* Shakespeare has revealed his themes to you, by explaining *how* his methods have allowed you to understand his meaning.

To help with your revision, you should also look at the sample questions available for all the new specifications, which can be found on the websites of each exam board. Try answering as many sample questions as you can. You could ask your teacher to look at your responses and give you some feedback on how well you have hit the Assessment Objectives (see p. 76).

There are many *Pause for thought* boxes throughout this guide that will encourage you to think more deeply about Shakespeare's intentions in writing *Romeo and Juliet*. It is only by developing a clear idea of this in your own head that you will be able to refer to the parts of the play that have made you interpret it in the way that you have. Remember that the examiner is all too aware that there is no such thing as a right or wrong answer in the study of literature — only well-argued or poorly argued opinions.

Different interpretations

The story of *Romeo and Juliet* has been adapted many times since its first staging during Shakespeare's day. An opera, a symphonic poem (Tchaikovsky) and several film versions of *Romeo and Juliet* have been produced, as well as other forms. There have also been many modern adaptations of the play, perhaps the best known being the musical production, *West Side Story*. This production features two young people who fall in love, not from rival families, but from rival gangs in the USA during the 1950s. As in the original play, the audience is invited to consider whether we may choose who we love, how hatred can divide and destroy people, and to what extent we (as opposed to outside forces such as fate or unlucky timing) are to blame for what happens to us.

Some examination boards (OCR and Edexcel) will ask you to write about films and other productions of the play. Remember, though, that the text itself is your primary focus. You will be asked to compare the original text to another production in order to evaluate how successfully you think the production has conveyed Shakespeare's intentions, or not, as the case may be.

Franco Zeffirelli's 1968 film attempts to capture the true feeling of the Verona in which Shakespeare set his play, while Baz Luhrmann's 1996 film places the production in a modern context in a high-energy, high-impact film. Both still use the original text, but the Luhrmann version heavily edits it with some cunning changes made, such as the word 'Sword' used as a manufacturer's name, appearing on the guns in Act 1 scene 1. You should also consider the way that characters are presented, asking yourself which aspects of Shakespeare's original text the producer's choices suggest they are trying to highlight. For example, consider the way in which the character of Mercutio is portrayed in Luhrmann's production and how this may reinforce an impression embedded in the language of the original play that Mercutio's feelings for Romeo go beyond simple friendship.

> **Pause for thought**
>
> Why have there been so many different interpretations of *Romeo and Juliet*? Consider whether this is a strength or a weakness of the play and why.

Context

- What does the term 'context' mean?
- How does the context of a play inform our understanding of it?
- What aspects of Elizabethan society particularly relate to this play?
- What moral and philosophical issues of this era does the play reflect?
- To what extent might Shakespeare be challenging certain attitudes and systems of belief present in his society?

The 'context' of a play means the surrounding factors that may have influenced what the author wrote. But don't forget that these same factors also affect how the play is received by audiences. Without an understanding of societal values at the time the play was written, we cannot be in a position to understand what it was that Shakespeare may have been reflecting upon in his play, or what he wished his audiences to consider.

Shakespeare

William Shakespeare was born in Stratford-upon-Avon in 1564 and was educated at the local grammar school. He married Anne Hathaway when he was 18. They had three children: Susanna, born in 1583, and twins, Hamnet and Judith, in 1585.

Shakespeare moved to London in about 1590 and was, by this time, a playwright and an actor. He lived mainly in London for about 20 years, writing most of his 37 plays there. Several of his plays may have been co-written with other playwrights and some were revised by other writers. It is not certain exactly how many of his plays were actually written just by Shakespeare and no one is ever likely to truly know.

Shakespeare died on 23 April 1616.

Modern Verona

Elizabethan England and Verona

The setting

There is little mention of Verona's customs or of the qualities of Verona itself beyond the generalised description, 'fair Verona', in the Prologue to the play. In fact, the social, moral and philosophical values presented in the attitudes of the characters in the play all mirror the attitudes of Elizabethan England. By setting the play in Verona, Shakespeare achieved two things. First, he widened the appeal of the play, increasing the numbers in his audiences. Second, he deflected any accusations of being critical of the society whose rules were set down by his principal patron, Queen Elizabeth I. This is not to be underestimated, as without the support of the monarch, the theatres, under constant threat of closure at the time, would have certainly been shut down sooner than they were.

Men and women

Patriarchal Verona reflects perfectly the degree to which men also held power in England, even though this was a society that was ruled by a queen. In the world of the play, it is the male heads of two wealthy families of similarly high social standing ('both alike in dignity') that are involved in a feud (a long-standing quarrel, usually based on a point of 'honour') that seems to have arisen out of nothing more than 'an airy word' (in other words, nothing much at all and not even worthy of specific explanation). This is not incidental. Shakespeare's point in not even stating the cause of the feud reflects the degree to which male pride and a sense of honour was exaggerated at this time, leading to all sorts of unnecessary violence and agitation.

The women we see in the play are of a lower status than their men. Lady Capulet and Lady Montague try to stop their husbands from fighting in Act 1 scene 1, yet they are ineffectual. At this time, to be manly was not to brook any form of insult, no matter how trivial. We see instances of this throughout the play and this is explored further in the sections of this guide covering *Characterisation* and *Themes*. What is important for us to understand at this stage is that in the sixteenth century, the behaviour of old Montague and Capulet and of the young, passionate and impetuous youths in the play, would have been seen as normal.

Shakespeare also uses *Romeo and Juliet* to explore the position of women. Juliet is strong-willed for a female of her time and much of her dialogue with the other characters shows this. At times she adopts a subservient role when forced to do so by her father, but she does defy him nevertheless. For example, in Act 4 scene 2, she tells her father that she has 'learnt…to repent the sin/Of disobedient opposition' and will from that time forward be 'ever ruled by [him]', yet she has already made her plans to do exactly the opposite.

From a production point of view, another factor to be aware of is that, in line with the narrow choices available to women at the time, females

> **Pause for thought**
>
> Juliet makes a promise to marry Paris that she has no intention of fulfilling. What do you think Shakespeare might be suggesting about the male dominance common in his society and how it affects the ways in which women behave towards men?

Context

were not allowed to perform on stage, so all the female roles were played by young boys whose voices had not yet broken. Current productions are, for this reason, often more explicit in the depiction of the love scenes in the play than the original performances would have been.

Superstition

Another important belief at this time that is widely reflected and questioned in the play is the force of superstition. England at this time was a primarily Christian (Protestant) society and the Elizabethans had a strongly external locus of control, i.e. a belief that what happens to you is dictated not by yourself but by outside forces that are stronger than you. At this time the vast majority of people believed not just in God but also in fate, destiny, fortune (luck) or the stars (astrology). Although most people believed in the existence of a greater power, debates took place at the highest levels of the church about the extent to which individuals had free will. These debates played an important role in the European Renaissance movement, which took place throughout the fifteenth century.

The common belief system provided a convenient way for people to relieve themselves of responsibility for their own actions. Shakespeare and other playwrights of his time who questioned the degree to which we might be able to command the uses of our own lives were unusual, and it is because the questions they raise in their plays are so timeless that they are still enjoyed today. Without this contextual knowledge, we lose much of what the play is about. Romeo, for example, has misgivings before going to the ball, saying:

> Some consequence yet hanging in the stars
> Shall bitterly begin his fearful date
> With this night's revels, and expire the term
> Of a despisèd life closed in my breast,
> By some vile forfeit of untimely death.   (1.4 107–11)

He is attributing the responsibility for what will happen to him to a force beyond himself and goes on to accept this entirely when he states, 'But he that hath the steerage of my course/Direct my sail!' Shakespeare is making it clear that Romeo believes the stars and some divine pilot are in charge of what will happen to him, rather than himself. In illustrating this to the audience he is doing no more than reflecting what most of them would have believed themselves. Religious and superstitious beliefs often merged for the Elizabethans and this is often reflected in the actions and words of other characters as well as Romeo, throughout the play.

Pause for thought

Look again at Act 1 scene 4 lines 107–11. What might Shakespeare be suggesting to his audience about the relationship between personal responsibility and belief systems? How might this affect levels of harmony and peace in society? To what extent do religious and superstitious beliefs still have the power to move people to violence today?

Our understanding and interpretation of the play depend entirely on our being aware of these Elizabethan attitudes and belief systems and it is interesting to compare them with our own. Remember that *Romeo and Juliet* is popular worldwide.

Source material

It is thought that *Romeo and Juliet* is based on Arthur Brooke's narrative poem 'The Tragicall History of Romeus and Juliet', but there is an Italian version of the story actually set in Verona that bears some similarity to Shakespeare's version. In the poem, Juliet is 16 rather than 13 and many of the characters in Shakespeare's play, in particular Mercutio, are entirely new creations. This is not uncommon. Many of Shakespeare's plays were based on existing literary works, and it may have helped to gain popularity with the paying public to create works in this way.

What is important to realise is that although Shakespeare took the seed of an idea from another source, in *Romeo and Juliet* he moves far beyond this source in creating complex characters with human (and timeless) motivations and weaves them all together into a tale that resonates even in the different society we live in today. It is, in short, a classic love story and is known as such throughout the world.

Elizabethan Theatre

The theatre was a popular place in the 1590s, attracting huge audiences of up to 3,000 at a time. Attending the theatre was unlike today. It was a rowdy occasion, with the crowds often responding verbally to events portrayed on stage. This would have made it necessary for Shakespeare to convey his themes over and over again, through as wide a range of means as possible, including characters, events, language, symbolism, and the structure of the play itself. (See Prologue and Chorus in the next section.)

In spite of its huge popularity, however, there was also much opposition to the theatre as many Puritans (a strict religious movement) believed it to be sinful. It was also seen by many as a health hazard, as the huge audiences it drew also brought with them the risk of spreading the dreaded bubonic plague of the day. The many attempts made to close the theatres down were prevented only by the royal family's great liking for it, and they continued to be open until 1642.

The Globe Theatre

Most of Shakespeare's plays were performed at the Globe Theatre, which is still located on the South Bank of the River Thames in London between Waterloo and London Bridge stations.

Context

The audience either stood in front of the stage (these people were called Groundlings and did not have to pay much to attend a play) or sat on hard wooden benches so a cushion was recommended (these were wealthier people who would have to pay more to be seated).

The Globe Theatre

Grade *focus*

In your study of *Romeo and Juliet*, depending on your exam board, you may need to show how your contextual knowledge has helped you to understand what Shakespeare is trying to say — his subtext. You will not gain marks by giving historical or biographical detail unlinked to details in the play itself. The examiners are interested only in how your contextual knowledge has helped you to interpret these details.

To obtain a grade C you are expected to formulate and express your own views with clarity and refer to some of the ways in which Shakespeare uses characters, events or language to reveal what was typical of the times he lived in. For example, you might comment on how women were expected to be subservient to their men and show how this is illustrated with reference to Lady Capulet, the Nurse and Juliet.

To gain an A* your writing has to go beyond simple clarity. Your argument must be more detailed, searching and convincing, with an excellent range of quotations skilfully embedded in your essay to illustrate your points. Your contextual knowledge should be evident throughout your essay in the way you refer to the society of the time in your explanation of the events, actions or language of the play. You are expected to reflect more deeply on Shakespeare's underlying meanings — his subtext — writing, for example, about the moral and philosophical suggestions that Shakespeare may have been making.

For example, you might speculate that Shakespeare questions the degree to which men *should* respond violently to a perceived insult and refer to his first scene where chaos ensues from the feud that we hear from Prince Escalus is 'bred of an airy word'. You might consider the significance of the Prince being called Escalus — a word meaning scales, a common symbol for the idea of justice. Equally, you might suggest that Shakespeare was a feminist who saw the oppression of women as harmful to the fabric of society as a whole, leading them merely to 'disobey' in private, as with Juliet and her secret marriage to Romeo. All of your speculations will need to be fully supported with short and relevant quotation and/or references to the text.

Review your learning

(Answers are given on p. 92.)
1. What is meant by the context of a play?
2. How can *Romeo and Juliet* be said to be a product of its time?
3. What use does Shakespeare make of Verona as a setting?

More interactive questions and answers online.

Plot and structure

- What are the main events of the play?
- How do the main storylines develop through the play?
- What is the time structure of the play?

The Prologue

The Prologue was just one device used by Shakespeare to ensure that his audience knew the basic plot line *before* the play commenced. Its concluding lines make this function clear:

> ...if you with patient ears attend,
> What here shall miss, our toil shall strive to mend

In other words, although the Elizabethan audience may have missed, or may have not actually been able to 'hear' what the Prologue has just outlined, the rest of the play will repeat and make it clearer. (See *Context* for further explanation of how noisy the Elizabethan theatre was.)

In addition to ensuring the audience's awareness of the central storyline from the start, the Prologue is a literary device that was used in Greek tragedy. Typically, a group of minor characters from the play, called the Chorus, acted as a means of communicating directly to the audience, often commenting on what was happening on the stage and making some kind of moral evaluation of the characters' thoughts, feelings and actions. Shakespeare limits his use of the Chorus to this Prologue and one other intervention at the start of Act 2, but it is important to note that he is giving away the end of the play right at the outset. This is not usual practice in the telling of a story. He does not do it at the beginning of all his plays, and these were also performed in the noisy Elizabethan theatres, so we must consider other reasons for why he does this.

Act 1 scene 1

- There is a street fight between members of the Capulet and Montague households.
- Romeo arrives in a melancholic mood and explains why he is so depressed.

The scene opens with two Capulet servants boasting that they are far better than the Montagues. Two of Montague's servants appear and the Capulet

---

Grade booster

To gain higher marks in the exam, you need to consider aspects of the play's form and structure — like the Prologue — and, particularly, how these inform the audience's understanding. In this case, the fact that Shakespeare gives the end away at the beginning, could be seen as a suggestion to the audience that the real tragedy of this play is not in what happens, but in *why* it happens.

Key quotation

What, drawn and talk of peace?
I hate the word,

As I hate hell, all Montagues, and thee.

Have at thee, coward.
(1.1 61–63)

Plot and structure

servants taunt them, trying to start a fight. One 'bites' their thumb at the Montague servants, an insult expressing hatred and contempt.

Benvolio, from the house of Montague, tries to calm everyone down. Tybalt, one of the Capulets, insults the Montagues even more, enjoying the chance to fight them.

The Prince stops the fight and chastises both Capulet and Montague, threatening them with death should either of them disturb the peace again.

When the crowds have dispersed, the Montagues ask Benvolio if he has seen Romeo and the conversation turns to Romeo's recent depression. Benvolio tells them he will attempt to discover its cause. The two meet and we learn that Romeo is passionately in love with a girl called Rosaline who does not return his love.

Romeo then notices signs of the fight and asks Benvolio what has happened, but then quickly adds, 'Yet tell me not, for I have heard it all'.

> **Pause for thought**
>
> Why do you think Shakespeare begins the play with a fight that escalates from a petty insult?
>
> What is the effect of Shakespeare putting a comma before the word 'coward' on the last line of Tybalt's speech (1.1 61–63)?

> **Pause for thought**
>
> Romeo says to Benvolio: 'Yet tell me not, for I have heard it all' and 'O any thing of nothing first create!' What point about the cause of the feud between the two households is Shakespeare reinforcing here through the character of Romeo?

Act 1 scene 2

- Paris and Capulet discuss Paris's potential marriage to Juliet.
- Romeo accepts Benvolio's challenge of going to Capulet's party, but only because Rosaline will be there and to prove Benvolio wrong.

Paris asks Capulet if he can marry his daughter, Juliet. At this early point in the play Capulet suggests that she is too young, having 'not seen the change of fourteen years'. Paris points out that 'Younger than she are happy mothers made' and Capulet responds with '…too soon marred are those so early made'.

Capulet sends his servant off with all the invitations to the party, but the servant can't read the names and gets Romeo to read them for him. Romeo discovers that Rosaline will be going to Capulet's party and Benvolio urges him to go as well so that he can prove that there are many more beautiful women than Rosaline.

> **Pause for thought**
>
> Shakespeare goes to great pains to point out to the audience just how deeply in love with Rosaline Romeo thinks he is. Why does he do this at this stage in the play? (Structure)

Text focus

> 'But woo her, gentle Paris, get her heart,
> My will to her consent is but a part;
> And she agreed, within her scope of choice
> Lies my consent and fair according voice.' (1.2 16–19)

Given that we have just learnt that it is the norm for girls not only to be married, but also to have had children by the time they are even younger than Juliet (13), what impression is Shakespeare giving us of Lord Capulet here? Does he seem to be a typical Elizabethan father? What exactly is he saying to Paris about Juliet and 'choice'?

Working with a partner, try paraphrasing this conversation (putting it into your own, modern language) between Paris and Capulet, starting from Paris's line, '…what say you to my suit?' and finishing with Capulet's '…makes my number more.'

When Romeo agrees to go to the Capulet party, Benvolio tells him:

> 'Compare her face with some that I shall show,
> And I will make thee think thy swan a crow.' (1.2 86–87)

How does the imagery (birds) used here help us understand Benvolio's point?

Romeo's response is:

> 'When the devout religion of mine eye
> Maintains such falsehood, then turn tears to fires;
> And these who, often drowned, could never die,
> Transparent heretics, be burnt for liars.' (1.2 88–91)

Here Romeo uses imagery relating to religion, witchcraft and heretics. (Those suspected of being witches were dunked — try doing an internet search for 'witches and dunking'. People who denied God, known as heretics, were burned alive.) Romeo has called his love for Rosaline the 'religion' of his eyes. What does he suggest might be done to him if he ever stops loving Rosaline?

Act 1 scene 3

- Lady Capulet, the Nurse and Juliet discuss Juliet's possible marriage to Paris.

Lady Capulet calls for her daughter, Juliet, before discussing with the Nurse how young she is. Lady Capulet asks Juliet what she thinks about getting married to Paris, saying many positive things about him. Juliet says she has not considered marriage yet but will be guided by her mother.

Plot and structure

> ### *Text* focus
>
> Juliet's response to her mother with regards to whether or not she can 'like' Paris, at this stage is:
>
> > 'I'll look to like, if looking liking move;
> > But no more deep will I endart mine eye
> > Than your consent gives strength to make it fly.'   (1.3 98–100)
>
> You will gain marks by being able to comment on why it is important that we hear Juliet say this to her mother *just before* she meets Romeo at the ball in the next scene. This placing side by side of certain things for effect is called **juxtapositioning**. Especially important are the words '…no more deep will I endart mine eye/Than your consent gives strength to make it fly'. Why? What does this suggest to the audience about Juliet's attitude towards her mother at this point? (Structure)

Act 1 scene 4

- Mercutio, Benvolio, Romeo and others wearing masks are preparing to go to Capulet's party.

Romeo is reluctant, having had a bad dream, but isn't given the opportunity to speak of it as Mercutio launches into a speech about dreams and 'Queen Mab', the fairy that races through the brains of those asleep and causes them to dream about specific things. His humorous tone changes though and becomes quite disturbed, as he transforms Queen Mab into a 'hag' and conjures brutal and quite degrading images of women in the act of sex.

Romeo appears concerned for his friend, telling him he talks of 'nothing', but then reveals his own bad feeling about going to the party. He is quite explicit here and suggests that he fears something will happen at this party over which he will have no control, but which will lead to his own 'untimely [meaning early] death'.

> ### *Text* focus
>
> What is the significance of this talk of 'dreams' and of Romeo's words below?
>
> > 'Some consequence yet hanging in the stars
> > Shall bitterly begin his fearful date
> > With this night's revels…
> > …But He that hath the steerage of my course,
> > Direct my sail!'   (1.5. 107–09, 112–13)
>
> How is our knowledge of what people believed at this time critical in helping us to understand what might be Shakespeare's point in these lines? (Context)

ROMEO AND JULIET

Act 1 scene 5

- The party at Capulet's house.
- Romeo and Juliet meet for the first time.

Romeo sees Juliet for the first time and instantly falls in love with her, not even pausing to consider that Benvolio has been right; Rosaline is history. Shakespeare even has Romeo use the same imagery as in Benvolio's earlier comment when he exclaims of Juliet, 'So shows a snowy dove trooping with crows,/As yonder lady o'er her fellows shows.'

Tybalt hears Romeo and is determined to kill him for daring to come to their party. Capulet urges Tybalt to leave Romeo alone, saying how Romeo is respected throughout Verona. Tybalt is not easily convinced until Capulet reminds him who is in charge, establishing his authority. Nevertheless, Tybalt makes clear that he is storing up his anger for a later date.

Romeo and Juliet meet each other. Juliet, too, falls immediately in love.

Text focus

Look again at some of the things Romeo and Juliet say to each other the first time they meet:

'If I profane with my unworthiest hand
This holy shrine, the gentle sin is this,
My lips, two blushing pilgrims, ready stand
To smooth that rough touch with a tender kiss.'   (1.5 92–95)

'Good pilgrim, you do wrong your hand too much,
Which mannerly devotion shows in this;
For saints have hands that pilgrims' hands do touch,
And palm to palm is holy palmers' kiss.'   (1.5 96–99)

Shakespeare uses a great deal of imagery here. Identify what imagery is used and what impression it gives us of how they feel about one another.

Key quotation

My only love sprung from my only hate!

Too early seen unknown, and known too late.
(1.5 137–38)

The Nurse intervenes and tells Juliet her mother wants to speak to her before revealing to Romeo that Juliet is a Capulet. This shocks Romeo, who realises the problems this could cause them both. Juliet asks the Nurse the name of the boy she has just kissed. When the Nurse tells her he is a Montague, she also realises she has fallen in love with her family's enemy.

Chorus

- The Chorus reminds the audience that Romeo has forgotten about Rosaline.

Plot and structure

> ### *Text* focus
>
> 'Now old desire doth in his death-bed lie,
> And young affection gapes to be his heir;
> That fair for which love groaned for and would die,
> With tender Juliet matched in now not fair.
> Now Romeo is beloved, and loves again,
> Alike bewitchèd by the charm of looks;'
>
> What point is Shakespeare using the Chorus to make about the nature of Romeo's love for Juliet?
>
> How does he use personification to help us to understand his meaning?
>
> Why do you think he gives these lines to the Chorus and not to one of the other characters, for example Benvolio, who has known of his 'love' for Rosaline? (See *Style* for more about Shakespeare's use of language and other literary devices.)

Act 2 scene 1

- Romeo hides in the gardens of the Capulet mansion.

Romeo doesn't want to leave the grounds of the house where Juliet is, so he stays and hides. His friends look for him, joking about his love for Rosaline, Mercutio again making crude jokes where he talks of women as sexual objects only. When Romeo won't come out from his hiding place, they go without him, but Mercutio is clearly disappointed.

> **Pause for thought**
>
> If Mercutio has 'never felt' the 'wound' of love, what does this suggest about his relationships with women?

Act 2 scene 2

- Romeo and Juliet tell one another of their feelings.
- They make plans for the future.

Romeo has overheard the conversation between Mercutio and Benvolio and states, 'He jests at scars that never felt a wound.'

Romeo sees Juliet and continues to speak aloud to himself about how beautiful she is, comparing her, as he does throughout the play, to things light and bright in nature. She speaks to the stars in heaven, while Romeo longs to be with her and to be able to touch her. When Juliet speaks she sighs because Romeo is a Montague and she is unhappy because his name will cause problems. However, she states that if he won't deny his name, as long as he loves her, she will quite happily stop being a Capulet.

When Juliet tells Romeo that if he is found he will be killed, he tells her that he is more frightened of her rejection than of death. Juliet worries that having overheard her talk of her love for him, Romeo will think her too easily won and will not value her because of this. Romeo fears that it is all a dream, 'Too flattering-sweet to be substantial' (real). She tells him

> **Pause for thought**
>
> Re-read Juliet's soliloquy at the window. How does this square with her words to her mother on being asked if she could 'like' Paris?

that if his love is 'honourable' and his 'purpose marriage', to send word to her the following day.

> **Pause for thought**
>
> Juliet tells Romeo:
>
> > …Although I joy in thee,
> > I have no joy of this contract tonight.
> > It is too rash, too unadvised, too sudden,
> > Too like the lightning which doth cease to be
> > Ere one can say 'It lightens'. (2.2 116–20)
>
> What aspect of their love do you think Shakespeare wants his audience to consider? How might this quality of their relationship relate to what we have already been told will become of them?

Act 2 scene 3

- Romeo goes to Friar Lawrence for advice about marrying Juliet.
- We are introduced to Friar Lawrence.

> **Text focus**
>
> Read the Friar's speech from 'Holy Saint Francis, what a change is here!' to 'Women may fall, when there's no strength in men' (2.3 65–80).
>
> What does the Friar mean when he says 'Young men's love then lies/Not truly in their hearts, but in their eyes.'

> **Key quotation**
>
> Wisely and slow, they stumble that run fast. (2.3 94)

Friar Lawrence looks out on the dawn rising and feels positive about the coming day, which is **ironic** when you consider what is about to happen. Shakespeare makes clear that he has a deep knowledge of herbs and potions, important for what is to come later. When Romeo arrives so early the Friar assumes he has been with Rosaline, thus we find out that Romeo confides more in the Friar than in his own parents who have earlier had to rely on Benvolio to try to find out why Romeo has been so out of spirits. When Romeo tells the Friar of his changed feelings the Friar responds at length.

Nevertheless, the Friar agrees to help Romeo marry Juliet because he hopes their marriage will end the feud between the Capulets and the Montagues, although he advises Romeo to take things slowly because rushing may result in problems.

Act 2 scene 4

- Mercutio blames Rosaline for Romeo's continued disappearance.
- He and Benvolio discuss a threatening letter that Tybalt has sent Romeo.
- Romeo arrives with his wits once more about him, which pleases Mercutio.
- The Nurse arrives to speak to Romeo and secretly plan a wedding between the young lovers.

Plot and structure

Mercutio and Benvolio are looking for Romeo, thinking he is still with Rosaline. Mercutio shows that his dislike of Rosaline stems from the alteration she has caused in Romeo's personality. They discuss a letter that Tybalt has sent, which challenges Romeo to a duel. Benvolio is certain Romeo will accept, but Mercutio suggests that he has been un-manned by Rosaline, 'stabbed with a white wench's black eye, run through the ear with a love-song…' and adds 'and is he a man to encounter Tybalt?'

However, when Romeo appears, he seems back to his old self. He and Mercutio have a battle of wits.

The Nurse arrives and tells Romeo that she hopes his intentions are honourable. She is easily satisfied, though she does admit to having suggested to Juliet that Paris would be a better match for her. They arrange for Juliet to be at Friar Lawrence's cell that afternoon where he will marry them.

Pause for thought

Mercutio states, 'Why, is not this better now than groaning for love?' How is this ironic? What does the audience know to be the cause of Romeo's restored wits?

Act 2 scene 5

- Juliet impatiently awaits news about Romeo.

Juliet is impatiently waiting at home for the Nurse to return. She thinks the Nurse is too slow and speculates on the reasons why she has not come back, thinking perhaps she has not met Romeo.

When she returns, the Nurse teases Juliet, praising Romeo's physical attractiveness, but making her wait for the news she wants to hear. At last she tells her of the plan, which Juliet receives with great joy.

Key quotation

Jesu, what haste! can you not stay awhile?
(2.5 29)

Grade *booster*

For higher marks, consider how the treatment of major themes alters over the course of the play. So far, love seems to have nothing to do with the inner characteristics of individuals, but everything to do with looks. What might Shakespeare be suggesting about this sort of love?

Act 2 scene 6

- Romeo and the Friar await Juliet.
- Romeo and Juliet go off to be married.

The Friar asks the heavens to look down and bless the marriage and hopes that it won't lead to later regrets. Romeo doesn't care what may be in store as long as he can call Juliet his.

Once Juliet has arrived the Friar takes them off to be married.

Key quotation

Therefore love moderately…
(2.6 14)

Text focus

Read the Friar's speech from 'These violent delights have violent ends,' to '…long love doth so' (2.6. 9–14). What metaphor does Shakespeare use here to suggest that we tire most quickly of what we find most delicious?

ROMEO AND JULIET

> **Pause for thought**
>
> The audience does not see the wedding between Romeo and Juliet. We are told it will be 'short work' (line 35) because the Friar does not want the lovers to be left alone until they are married: 'you shall not stay alone/Till Holy Church incorporate two in one.' What might this suggest about the marriage?

Act 3 scene 1

- The second fight takes place.
- Mercutio is killed.
- Romeo kills Tybalt in revenge and is banished.

> **Key quotation**
>
> The day is hot, the Capels are abroad,
>
> And if we meet we shall not scape a brawl,
>
> For now, these hot days, is the mad blood stirring.
>
> (3.1 2–4)

> **Pause for thought**
>
> If Benvolio and Mercutio had gone inside then none of the following events would have occurred. Or would they have just occurred at another time? What part does fate play in this scene and in the rest of the play?

Benvolio, the voice of reason, urges Mercutio to go inside and away from a potential brawl with the Capulets.

The Capulets arrive and when Tybalt asks to speak to them, Mercutio antagonises him. Tybalt suggests that Mercutio is Romeo's 'consort', a word meaning wife or husband. This may be a simple insult casting doubt on Mercutio's manliness, or you may see an insinuation that the two have a relationship that goes beyond platonic friendship. Mercutio is ready to fight Tybalt over this, but when Romeo arrives, Tybalt immediately turns his attention to his original target and insults Romeo by calling him a 'villain'. This would have been an insult that no red-blooded Elizabethan (or Renaissance Italian) youth would have been expected to take without a fight.

Instead, to Mercutio's horror, Romeo says he loves Tybalt, though he can't explain why to him at the moment. Mercutio cannot stand by and watch his friend disgrace himself so draws his sword to fight Tybalt.

> **Pause for thought**
>
> 'O calm, dishonourable, vile submission!' (3.1 66)
>
> How does our knowledge of codes of honour at this time help us to understand Mercutio's response here? (Context)

Romeo tries to calm the situation down and to stop the fight but, by getting in the way, causes Mercutio to be fatally stabbed.

Mercutio tries to laugh off his wound as 'Ay, ay, a scratch, a scratch' (line 85) but he knows it is enough to kill him. He expresses his frustration at the feud, which he sees as the reason for his untimely death:

Plot and structure

A plague a' both houses! I am sped. (3.1 83)

Romeo vows to avenge Mercutio's death by killing Tybalt but the minute after he has done so, sees himself as the victim of bad luck. Benvolio persuades him to flee from the scene.

The Prince arrives and Benvolio honestly tells him what has happened. Lady Capulet rushes on, sees the dead Tybalt and demands a revenge killing from the Prince. She accuses Benvolio of lying, showing how close she was to Tybalt. Montague reminds the Prince that in killing Tybalt, Romeo has merely concluded 'but what the law should end,/The life of Tybalt', as it was he who killed Mercutio. It is also revealed that Mercutio was the Prince's own kinsman. As a compromise, Romeo is banished but had better go 'in haste', as if he is found he will be killed.

> **Pause for thought**
>
> When Mercutio dies, he doesn't blame fate, the stars or fortune for what happens to him, but lays the blame squarely at the feet of the Capulets and Montagues.
>
> How does this compare to how others in the play react to what happens to them?
>
> Why do you think Shakespeare creates this contrast?
>
> What characteristics of Mercutio make his death a sad loss to the audience?

> **Key quotation**
>
> O, I am fortune's fool! (3.1 127)

Act 3 scene 2

- Juliet hears of Romeo's banishment.
- The Nurse comforts her by telling her she will find Romeo and bring him to her.

Juliet is looking forward to spending the night with Romeo when the Nurse arrives with news of the events in the square, making it sound as if Romeo is dead. When Juliet discovers the truth, she feels betrayed by Romeo.

> **Text focus**
>
> 'O serpent heart, hid with a flow'ring face!
> Did ever dragon keep so fair a cave?
> Beautiful tyrant, fiend angelical!
> Dove-feathered raven, wolvish-ravening lamb!
> Despisèd substance of divinest show!
> Just opposite to what thou justly seems't
> A damnèd saint, an honourable villain.' (3.2 73–79)
>
> How does Shakespeare use language here to reveal Juliet's thoughts about Romeo?

> **Key quotation**
>
> 'Romeo is banishèd,' to speak that word,
> Is father, mother, Tybalt, Romeo, Juliet,
> All slain, all dead.
> 'Romeo is banishèd!' (3.2 122–24)

When she has reconciled herself to the death of her cousin, realising that he would have killed Romeo if Romeo had not killed him, she mourns

ROMEO AND JULIET 21

the fact that she will not be able to enjoy her husband in the physical sense as he has been banished.

Juliet says she will die a virgin and seems intent on killing herself at this point. The Nurse offers Juliet some hope by saying that she knows where Romeo is and will get him to come to her that night to comfort her.

Act 3 scene 3

- Friar Lawrence tells Romeo he has been banished.
- Romeo responds to this just as Juliet has.
- The Friar upbraids him for ingratitude.

The Friar tries to see the positive side, saying 'the world is broad and wide', but Romeo sees his banishment as a death as he will be separated from Juliet. The Friar is annoyed that Romeo is ungrateful for being saved. He tells him that normally his crime would have resulted in death, but the Prince has been 'kind' to him. This does not convince Romeo, who sees it as 'torture' because here is 'heaven' as this is 'Where Juliet lives'.

The Nurse arrives on an 'errand' for Juliet. She sees Romeo weeping on the ground and criticises him for acting pathetically:

> Stand up, stand up, stand, and you be a man:
> For Juliet's sake, for her sake, rise and stand; (3.3 88–89)

Romeo is worried that Juliet now thinks less of him and attempts to kill himself. The Friar tells him to calm down and accuses him of being like a woman or a 'beast'.

Pause for thought

> 'Thy tears are womanish, thy wild acts denote
> The unreasonable fury of a beast.' (3.3 110–11)

What message about Elizabethan values can we draw from Romeo being described *negatively* as 'womanish' and an 'unreasonable…beast' in the same sentence?

The Friar reminds Romeo of the reasons why he should be happy:
- Juliet is alive.
- His enemy, who wanted to kill him (Tybalt), is dead.
- He is banished and not sentenced to death.

He tells him to cheer up, go to Juliet and comfort her, without staying too long. The Friar then makes future plans: Romeo will go to Mantua and wait there until the Friar can find a way of publicising their marriage and reconciling the families.

Key quotation

Ha, banishment? be merciful, say 'death';

For exile hath more terror in his look,

Much more than death. Do not say 'banishment'!

(3.3 12–14)

Pause for thought

Is Romeo's behaviour in this scene a realistic portrayal of an adolescent?

What might Shakespeare be warning his audience of?

Act 3 scene 4

- Capulet brings forward the marriage of Juliet to Paris.
- Paris is delighted.
- Capulet has no doubts at all that Juliet will fall in happily with his plans.

Capulet tells Paris that he has not been able to talk to Juliet about how she might feel towards him as she is mourning the death of her cousin. He appears to think again though and speaks for Juliet, saying that he will make a 'desperate tender' of her love to him. What this means is that he is offering her love to Paris. It is **ironic** and even a little comic, that he then states:

> …I think she will be ruled
> In all respects by me; nay more, I doubt it not.   (3.4 13–14)

It is the early hours of the morning and he instructs Lady Capulet to go and see Juliet before going to her bed, to tell her about the intended marriage to Paris.

Pause for thought

Remember that Juliet is 13 years old. Capulet has just lost considerable face in front of the Prince whose kinsman has been murdered by one of his family. Paris, we know, is of exceptionally high status in Verona. What might this tell us about the role of marriage in this society?

Act 3 scene 5

- Romeo and Juliet part after a night together.
- Capulet tells Juliet she will marry Paris.
- Juliet plans to visit Friar Lawrence to beg for his help in finding a way out of the situation.

Romeo and Juliet have just spent the night together and it is time for Romeo to leave. Juliet begs Romeo to stay longer. Romeo assures her it is dawn and that he must leave as they have heard the morning lark and he can see the glow of dawn in the sky.

The Nurse arrives to warn Juliet that her mother is coming to her bedroom, the dawn has broken and that Romeo needs to be careful.

Juliet pleads with Romeo to send her messages every day. As they part, Juliet tells Romeo:

> O God, I have an ill-divining soul!
> Methinks I see thee, now thou art so low,
> As one dead in the bottom of a tomb.
>   (3.5 54–56)

Leonard Whiting as Romeo and Olivia Hussey as Juliet in Zeffirelli's 1968 adaptation

Grade booster

This scene is actually the last time Juliet sees Romeo alive. Remember that the audience has been told in the Prologue that they will both die at the end of the play. Being able to observe the pathos (an appeal to the audience's sympathy) of this foreshadowing of events, will gain you higher marks in your assessment.

> **Grade *booster***
>
> Commenting on context and the complexities of Shakespeare's presentation of issues of his day will help improve your grade. Arranged marriages were common in sixteenth-century Britain and this scene highlights how the issue is a difficult one, with the parents believing strongly that they are acting in the best interests of their daughter and the family name.

Lady Capulet tells Juliet the details of the planned wedding. Juliet is adamant she will not marry Paris. Capulet arrives and sees Juliet crying. Lady Capulet tells him that Juliet will not marry Paris.

Capulet leaves Juliet in no doubt that she will be forced to marry Paris next Thursday. He threatens to throw Juliet out of his house if she refuses to marry Paris:

> And you be mine, I'll give you to my friend;
> And you be not, hang, beg, starve, die in the streets,   (3.5 191–92)

Here 'and' means 'if'. Capulet is saying that either Juliet accepts that she is his possession, in which case she also accepts that he can 'give' her to whomever he wishes, or she insists that she doesn't 'belong' to him and she goes her own way with no help from him.

> **Pause for thought**
>
> Read Capulet's threat in lines 191–92 again.
>
> In the context of the times, how could a girl of this class, not brought up to work, survive without her father or a husband?
>
> Do Capulet's words and actions give us some insight into why there are problems between the Capulets and the Montagues?
>
> Does it help to explain why Juliet has married Romeo so quickly?

> **Grade *booster***
>
> Elevate your grade by suggesting that through scenes such as this, Shakespeare is making some kind of social comment. Here, perhaps he is commenting on the negative affects on society of oppressive male attitudes towards women. Deceit becomes entirely acceptable to women, even to the point of expressly disobeying the ruling of the church.

Juliet is devastated by this turn of events and turns to her mother for help, threatening to kill herself if the marriage is not delayed. Her mother will have nothing more to do with her however. (See *Characterisation* for further exploration of this.) Even the Nurse appears to see nothing wrong with Juliet committing bigamy and marrying Paris, so long as it isn't found out.

Once the Nurse has gone, Juliet reveals her true plans and feelings in a **soliloquy** (where a character speaks their own thoughts aloud to the audience). She quite coolly casts the Nurse off, saying she will have nothing more to do with her and vows that if the Friar cannot help her, she will kill herself.

Act 4 scene 1

- Paris visits the Friar regarding marriage arrangements between himself and Juliet.
- Juliet finds him there with the Friar.
- Paris leaves and Juliet tells the Friar of her resolve to kill herself if he can't help her to avoid the marriage.

Plot and structure

Paris is visiting Friar Lawrence to tell him about his plans to marry Juliet. The Friar is understandably surprised and tells him 'the time is very short', but Paris explains that it is to help Juliet to overcome her grief at Tybalt's death.

When Juliet arrives, Paris greets her as his 'lady' and 'wife' and she responds with a double entendre (something that can mean two different things) that Paris does not understand, but the audience does:

> That may be, sir, when I may be a wife. (4.1 19)

However, Paris continues to press the point that she has no choice and even suggests that she should not 'mar' (mess up) her face by crying so much (he thinks over Tybalt's death) as it is now '[his] face'. Shakespeare is reinforcing the point that Paris sees her as a possession, just as her father does. The interesting thing to note here is that Shakespeare doesn't give Paris any awareness that his attitude might be offensive to Juliet.

When Paris leaves, at first the Friar states that he knows of no remedy. When Juliet threatens suicide, he can 'spy a kind of hope' in her desperation, telling her that if she would be prepared to die in reality, perhaps she might be prepared to take a potion that would make her appear dead.

> **Pause for thought**
>
> Look again at Juliet's response in line 19. What does Paris think she means? What is Juliet's other meaning?
>
> How has Juliet learned to cope with male dominance in her life?

Text focus

How does Shakespeare use comparison in the passage below to make it clear to us that Juliet is resolved not to marry Paris? Re-write the numbered items in your own words, making clear what Juliet is saying she would do rather than marry Paris.

> [1] 'O bid me leap, rather than marry Paris,
> From off the battlements of yonder tower,
> [2] Or walk in thievish ways, [3] or bid me lurk
> Where serpents are; [4] chain me with roaring bears,
> [5] Or shut me nightly in a charnel-house,
> O'ercover'd quite with dead men's rattling bones,
> With reeky shanks and yellow chapless skulls;
> [6] Or bid me go into a new-made grave
> And hide me with a dead man in his shroud…'
>
> (4.1 77–85)

> **Pause for thought**
>
> Why is the comment, 'Or bid me go into a new-made grave/And hide me with a dead man in his shroud…' particularly ironic?

The Friar instructs Juliet to go home and to pretend to give consent to marry Paris. The potion she takes will make her seem dead. This will last for 42 hours. He sends another friar to Mantua with a letter telling Romeo of the plan so that Romeo will be by her side when she awakes.

Act 4 scene 2

- The final wedding plans are made.
- Juliet tells her father that she is sorry for her disobedience.

Though short, this scene is filled with **irony**. Capulet is forging ahead with the marriage plans when Juliet returns from the Friar and kneels before him. She tells him:

> …I have learnt me to repent the sin
> Of disobedient opposition
> To you and your behests…
> Henceforward I am ever ruled by you.   (4.2 16–21)

We know that as the play has progressed, Juliet has 'learned' how to do precisely the opposite — to evade his 'behests' and to follow her own course. She has learned the art of subterfuge (being sneaky and hiding her true intentions under a cloak of deceit).

The **irony** is heightened further in Capulet's loaded remark:

> Now, afore God, this reverend holy friar,
> All our whole city is much bound to him.   (4.2 30–31)

The wedding day is then brought forward to Wednesday by a remark that Juliet makes. It could be considered that this is a double ruse (trick). First, her father will think her eager to marry Paris and so any suspicion of her trying to wriggle out of the marriage will be deflected. Second, she will be able to undergo her ordeal more quickly rather than having another day and night to think over the horror of what she is about to undertake.

Act 4 scene 3

- Juliet takes the potion.

Juliet asks the Nurse to leave her alone for the night, telling her she has to pray to free herself from sin. Alone, Juliet speculates as to whether the potion will work or if it might be a deadly poison that the Friar has given to her to save himself from the dishonour of having to marry her to Paris when he has already married her to someone else. She drinks the potion, toasting Romeo as she does.

Act 4 scene 4

- The wedding preparations continue.

> **Pause for thought**
>
> Juliet lies to her father but the audience knows her true intention. How is Shakespeare inviting the audience to reflect upon the results of an oppressive upbringing? Do you think he approves of this treatment of young women? Could it be argued that Shakespeare may have been something of a feminist?

> **Pause for thought**
>
> Act 4 scene 4 is a short scene but Shakespeare has included it for a reason. What point, or points, might Shakespeare be reinforcing here about Capulet? Consider the context: attitudes towards women; his earlier loss of face with the Prince of Verona; the importance of 'honour' to the idea of being a man; how do these contextual factors help us to understand what Shakespeare might be saying here?
>
> Now think about the structural reasons for having such a scene. What comes immediately before and after it? How will the audience respond to this kind of scene?

Plot and structure

Lady Capulet and the Nurse continue to prepare for the wedding. Capulet urges everyone to hurry up as there isn't much time and everything must be ready. He seems excited and in a positive frame of mind.

Capulet then sees Paris arrive and asks the Nurse to go and wake Juliet.

Act 4 scene 5

- Juliet is found 'dead'.

The Nurse goes to wake Juliet and, thinking that she is dead, alerts everyone. Lady Capulet seems genuinely distraught at the loss of her daughter saying that Juliet was the 'one thing' she had 'to rejoice and solace in', highlighting further how unhappy her marriage is.

The Friar calms them all down, urging them not to weep for her, as she is in a higher, better place. The Friar tells them to prepare to follow the body of Juliet to her grave. He uses their superstition to urge them to irritate heaven no more by being so sad.

Text focus

Read Capulet's words to Paris about Juliet's death:

'O son, the night before thy wedding day
Hath Death lain with thy wife. There she lies,
Flower as she was, deflowerèd by him.
Death is my son-in-law, Death is my heir.'

(4.5 35–38)

How has Shakespeare used personification here to suggest that even in death, Juliet isn't free from being considered as anything more than a male possession? What does this speech tell us about Capulet's priorities?

Act 5 scene 1

- Romeo is given the news that Juliet is dead.
- He decides to return to Verona to kill himself by Juliet's side.

This is the first time we have seen Romeo for some time. He has had another dream:

> My dreams presage some joyful news at hand. (5.1 2)

Romeo has dreamt that Juliet finds him dead but brings him back to life with a kiss.

Balthasar arrives from Verona with news of Juliet's death, saying that as soon as he saw her placed in the tomb he came to tell Romeo.

Romeo, devastated by this news, prepares to return to see Juliet one final time. As usual, Romeo acts on impulse and does not consider that the wise thing to do would be to go to the Friar before taking any further action. The audience knows that the Friar has sent a letter to Romeo

Pause for thought

Romeo's dream is clearly ironic. Why?

Romeo has many dreams in the play. What are they about and how does he react to them? What does his tendency to dream reveal to the audience about the amount of control he has over his own life?

Pause for thought

The late arrival of the Friar's letter is one of a number of misfortunes that happen to Romeo and Juliet throughout the play.

Make a list of the things that happen to Romeo and Juliet in the play that might be called unlucky. In every case, could these happenings also be explained as the results of human causes?

telling him of the plan relating to Juliet, but it does not seem to have arrived yet.

Romeo visits an apothecary (chemist) and pays him a lot of money for 'A dram of poison' which he determines to take and die by Juliet's side.

Act 5 scene 2

- Friar Lawrence discovers that Romeo has not received the letter.

Friar Lawrence asks Friar John whether he has a message or a letter for him from Romeo. Friar John tells him that he has been unable to see Romeo because he was prevented from going to Mantua. The Friar curses fortune, as the letter contained details of his plan.

The Friar decides to take dramatic action to prevent disaster. He resolves to be at the tomb when Juliet awakes and vows to write again to Mantua, so that Romeo will know what has happened. He will keep Juliet at his place, hidden, until Romeo returns for her.

Pause for thought
The Friar is quick to accept the idea of bad luck here as a cause of what could (at this stage of the play) be a disaster. What other cause for this disaster could Shakespeare have had the Friar reflecting upon here? Why do you think he doesn't?

Act 5 scene 3

Paris, grief stricken, has also gone to mourn his loss outside the tomb where Juliet lies. Romeo arrives with Balthasar and gives him a letter to take to his father. He then tells Balthasar to leave, but instead, he hides and witnesses what Romeo does next. Shakespeare has Romeo personify the earth that holds Juliet as a pregnant woman, whose womb holds not life, but death:

Juliet's 'deathbed' in the 1996 Luhrmann adaptation

> Thou detestable maw, thou womb of death,
> Gorged with the dearest morsel of the earth,
>
> (5.3 45–46)

As he opens the tomb Paris comes forward to challenge Romeo, thinking he has come to do something terrible to the dead bodies. He calls him 'vile Montague!' (line 54) reminding the audience of the feud which has contributed to the tragic events of the play. They fight and Romeo kills Paris. It is only at this point that Paris reveals his face, which devastates Romeo, showing his compassionate and good nature. He places Paris in the tomb near Juliet as a fitting tribute to someone else caught up in the terrible tragedy.

Romeo talks of his feelings, observing how beautiful Juliet looks even though she is dead, which is **ironic** as we know that she is not dead.

Plot and structure

Taking Juliet in his arms and kissing her one last time, he takes the poison, which has an immediate effect:

> ...O true apothecary!
> Thy drugs are quick. Thus with a kiss I die.   (5.3 119–20)

At this exact moment Friar Lawrence arrives, enters the tomb and, finding Romeo and Paris dead, curses time that allowed this to happen.

At this point, Juliet wakes up and asks for Romeo, but before the Friar can tell her what has happened they hear a noise and he urges her to come with him, away from such a terrible place. Juliet, seeing Romeo, refuses to leave. The Friar flees, worried that he will be found there: 'I dare no longer stay' (5.3 159).

Juliet guesses how Romeo has died and kisses him in the hope that there is enough poison on his lips to kill her as well. This does not work, so she kills herself quickly with a dagger before the watchmen can prevent her. She falls on Romeo's body, a symbol of their final unity.

Balthasar and the Friar are captured as the Prince, Capulet and Lady Capulet arrive to find out what has happened. Montague arrives with news that his wife has died due to the shock of Romeo's exile.

The Prince urges no one to make any more comments until they can discover what has happened. The Friar now tells the story of what happened, although it seems he is doing it to plead his innocence.

The letter that Shakespeare has had Romeo give to Balthasar is an important device as it tells everyone what Romeo had intended to do.

The Prince directs all his anger at Capulet and Montague and tells them that their conflict has caused this blood bath. He tells them that 'All are punished': no one is free from punishment from 'heaven', as if there is a moral message to be gained from all of this. It seems too late now, but this makes Capulet take Montague's hand and end the feud. Montague tells Capulet he will have a gold statue of Juliet made and Capulet responds by saying he will place a similar one of Romeo by her side.

The Prince is the last to speak, a tradition Shakespeare had of letting the highest-ranking character left alive have the final words. He summarises the terrible events that have occurred. The ending is gloomy, in terms of the many deaths, but there is some hope for the future as the feud is over.

The passage of time

The events of the play take place over just four days. This shows the haste of Romeo and Juliet's love and is a reason for the tragedy, showing that a little more calm and thought may have prevented the problems.

Key quotation

Death, that hath sucked the honey of thy breath,

Hath had no power yet upon thy beauty:
(5.3 92–93)

Pause for thought

First the Friar has blamed 'fortune' and now he blames time. To what extent is timing to blame: if messages had arrived on time, if Romeo had met Juliet at another time, if only the Friar had arrived a few minutes earlier?

Timeline

SUNDAY

Act 1 scene 1
Street brawl — Sunday 9 a.m. (line 152)

Act 1 scene 5
Capulet's party — Sunday evening

MONDAY

Act 2 scenes 1–3
Sunday night to Monday morning
Romeo outside Juliet's bedroom
The Friar watching dawn in his cell

Act 2 scene 6
Romeo and Juliet marry — Monday afternoon

Act 3 scene 1
Later Monday afternoon — fight with Tybalt

Act 3 scene 4
Late Monday night — Romeo and Juliet are together

TUESDAY

Act 3 scene 5
Tuesday dawn — Romeo leaves and immediately afterwards Juliet's mother, who has not yet been to bed, informs her of the planned wedding between her and Paris

Act 4 scene 2
Juliet's marriage is brought forward from Thursday to Wednesday

Act 4 scene 3
Juliet takes the potion

WEDNESDAY

Act 4 scene 5
Wednesday morning — Juliet is found 'dead'

Act 5 scene 1
Wednesday — day — Romeo leaves Mantua to return

Wednesday evening/night — Romeo returns to the grave, fights Paris and kills himself. Juliet wakes and kills herself

THURSDAY

Act 5 Scene 3
Dawn breaks on Thursday morning as the Prince sums up events

Plot and structure

Grade *focus*

In the examination you will not be rewarded for re-telling the story. Instead, you will be expected to explore the whys and wherefores of what happens in the play (the subtext).

C-grade answers:
- answer the question throughout
- refer to the play all the way through and make comments on Shakespeare's ideas
- use textual details, including quotations, all the way through
- explain the effects of the language, form or structure that Shakespeare uses
- make some appropriate comments on themes/ideas/settings

A*-grade answers:
- make insightful comments in a sharply focused argument linked closely to the question and the text throughout
- offer a range of carefully selected quotations and references that support and illustrate the argument
- evaluate aspects of Shakespeare's use of language, structure and form, interpreting the possible effects of these on audiences, past and present. This might include an evaluation of the use of imagery, the structure (e.g. order of presentation of events) that Shakespeare uses, or consider how the form of the text — a play — engages the recipient (audience) more personally than would, for example, a novel or a poem
- include a convincing and/or imaginative interpretation of ideas/themes/settings

Review your learning

(Answers are given on p. 92.)

1. Sum up the ten most important events of the play.
2. How are Benvolio and Tybalt important to the plot?
3. How is the relationship between Romeo and Juliet central to the play?
4. How does the ending of the play reflect the opening?

More interactive questions and answers online.

Characterisation

- What is each character like? What do they want?
- How does Shakespeare reveal the characters to us?
- What evidence can we find to help us think about each character?
- What are the relationships between characters?

It is important to note that when writing your answer it is impossible to separate the author's use of characterisation from the themes of the play. The examples given below integrate both characters and themes throughout.

Romeo

Romeo is the archetypal young lover. In fact, the expression 'a real Romeo' is still used to describe someone whose whole being revolves around the love of women and the expression of this love. The first we hear about Romeo is when Benvolio tells Lady Montague that he has seen him out early in the morning acting strangely. He is sad and depressed the first time he speaks: 'Ay me, sad hours seem long' (1.1 152).

Leonardo DiCaprio (left) as Romeo in the Luhrmann film

Characterisation

This is typical of Romeo, who reacts in a highly emotional manner to many events in the play. He has locked himself in his room and has been behaving out of character, according to Mercutio and Benvolio, who make light of the reason for his sadness, which is that the woman he loves, Rosaline, does not love him. When he is happily in love with Juliet in Act 2 he becomes more quick-witted and humorous. This emphasises Romeo's tendency to be extreme in the way that he reacts to anything that happens to him throughout the play.

When the others are excited about going to Capulet's party, Romeo refuses to dance and wants to be miserable on his own:

> …I have a soul of lead
> So stakes me to the ground I cannot move.   (1.4 15–16)

Grade *booster*

Higher grade answers will consider Shakespeare's structural and thematic intention in giving certain characters certain speeches. Romeo feels a sense of dread or doom before the Capulets' party. Shakespeare is preparing the audience for future terrible events and it is fitting that it is Romeo who feels this dread, as he is one of the central figures in the tragedy.

Romeo tells the others that he has had a premonition that the night's events will end in death. He talks of his dreams again at the start of Act 5, which shows he is influenced by superstitious beliefs.

When he sees Juliet for the first time he is mesmerised by her instantly, which seems fickle after his depression over Rosaline. This shows Romeo is passionate and extreme in his emotional responses. This impression is heightened by Shakespeare through the language Romeo uses in speaking of and to Juliet.

Romeo certainly seems in earnest about his feelings for Juliet. However, the swiftness with which he transfers his affections from one girl to another might lead an audience to wonder whether what he is feeling is love or merely infatuation. His lack of restraint highlights his impetuous nature and hints at the potential in his character to behave in a 'rash' and thoughtless manner.

However this might be, we learn that he is well thought of in Verona in general terms. When Tybalt wants to confront him at Capulet's party, Capulet states:

> …to say truth, Verona brags of him
> To be a virtuous and well-governed youth.   (1.5 66–67)

Pause for thought

Romeo is depressed about the situation with Rosaline, yet by the middle of Act 1 scene 5 he has fallen deeply in love with Juliet. What does this tell you about Romeo's character?

Pause for thought

Throughout the play, Romeo reveals his belief that his life is ruled by forces over which he has no control. Make a list of quotations from Romeo's speeches that support this view. What do you think Shakespeare wants us to feel about Romeo as a result of this?

Text focus

Look again at Romeo's words about Juliet from: 'But soft, what light through yonder window breaks?' to 'That I might touch that cheek!' (2.2 2–24)

How do the individual words and images that Shakespeare gives to Romeo here highlight the exact nature and quality of Romeo's love for Juliet?

ROMEO AND JULIET

> **Key quotation**
>
> Ha, banishment? be merciful, say 'death':
> (3.3 12)

> **Pause for thought**
>
> Apart from Romeo's character, what other factors do you think Shakespeare wishes us to consider play a role in the tragic outcomes of the play? Make a list.

> **Grade booster**
>
> To increase your marks, consider the language that Shakespeare gives to Romeo and how this reveals the degree to which he accepts responsibility for his own actions and their consequences.

When confronted with violence in Act 3 scene 1, Romeo tries to calm the situation down. His attempts to stop the fight result in Mercutio's death as he gets in the way. As with his feelings when in love, Romeo's feelings of violence are also strong, and he kills the seemingly powerful Tybalt easily.

When he hears he is to be banished he once again reacts in an extreme manner, telling the Friar that banishment is worse than death as he will be separated from Juliet.

The Friar berates (tells off) Romeo for his reaction, telling him that normally his crime would have resulted in death, and the Prince has therefore been 'kind' to him. This does not convince Romeo who sees it as 'torture' (line 29) because here is 'heaven' as this is 'where Juliet lives'. His behaviour in this section is childish and he refuses to see reason, seemingly rolling about on the floor crying, according to the Nurse.

Similarly, in Act 5 when he discovers Juliet is dead he rushes back to Verona to kill himself and be by her side. A little more patience and an attempt to communicate with the Friar could have resulted in a happy ending. Romeo's impetuous behaviour can be considered a leading cause in many of the key events in the play:

- the hasty and illicit wedding with Juliet
- the death of Mercutio
- the play's tragic conclusion

However, though Shakespeare seems to suggest that Romeo's character does contribute to the tragedy, there are clearly other factors that have a role to play.

Juliet

Juliet's character appears to change gradually throughout the play and, as a result, so does our view of her. At the beginning of the play she is portrayed as an innocent girl whom her father, Capulet, is protective of as she is only 13 years old.

> **Key quotation**
>
> My child is yet a stranger in the world,
> She hath not seen the change of fourteen years;
> (1.2 8–9)

Juliet is presented as obedient to her mother in her first scene, Act 1 scene 3, when she says: 'Madam, I am here.

Claire Danes as Juliet in the Luhrmann film

Characterisation

What is your will?' (line 7). She is described by the Nurse as 'the prettiest babe that e'er I nursed' (1.3 61), adding to the idea of Juliet's beauty and preparing the audience for Romeo's reaction to seeing her for the first time.

Juliet, at the beginning of the play, appears to be subservient to her parents, but she does not instantly agree to marry Paris when her mother mentions the possibility to her in Act 1 scene 3. The moment she sees Romeo, any feelings of uncertainty about marrying disappear. The fact that Juliet does not object to Romeo's advances and is attracted to him, to the point where she actually encourages him, is an example of her growing self-confidence as the play progresses and shows the depth of her passionate attraction to Romeo.

In Act 2 scene 5 Juliet shows signs of impatience when she waits at home for the Nurse to return.

Juliet shows further impatience when the Nurse appears in Act 3 scene 2 to tell her of the events of the previous scene. The banishment of Romeo, to Juliet, is worse than anything else she can think of, showing the depth of her feelings for him.

Juliet is adamant she will not marry Paris. One reason for this is because she is already married to Romeo, another is her headstrong nature. Remember that an Elizabethan audience would have seen her lack of subservience to her father as unusual behaviour for a young female. Her unconventional behaviour is further exemplified when she does not dutifully obey her father's wishes in Act 3 scene 5 and goes to desperate measures to avoid marrying a man she does not wish to marry.

She can be seen as quite manipulative, whether when trying to persuade Romeo to stay longer in Act 3 scene 5 or in the way she tries to play her mother and father off each other in Act 3 scene 5:

> O sweet my mother, cast me not away!
> Delay this marriage for a month, a week, (3.5 198–99)

She desperately tries to use her mother as a way of softening her father's resolution to throw her out of the family home if she does not marry Paris.

Juliet is clever with her dialogue when speaking to Paris. The quick-fire, witty dialogue in Act 4 scene 1 shows that while Juliet is not prepared to criticise Paris openly, she is hinting at the fact that she does not love him.

In Act 4 scene 2 she lies and tells her father she has repented 'the sin of disobedient opposition'. She mainly tells him the truth: Friar Lawrence has told her to do this, so it was not a lie that she has invented herself. She can be seen as a victim of

Pause for thought

What is it about Juliet that many of the other characters remark upon as making her special? What were men looking for in a woman at this time? How does Shakespeare's presentation of Juliet highlight what the ideal of 'perfection' in a woman was at this time?

Key quotation

But my true love is grown to such excess I cannot sum up sum of half my wealth.
(2.6 33–34)

Pause for thought

What does Juliet's impatience in Act 2 scene 5 serve to emphasise?

Grade booster

The presentation of Juliet could reveal Shakespeare's disapproval of a society in which the repression of women teaches them to become manipulative and sly, neither of which are particularly attractive qualities. This sort of speculation of possible authorial intention is necessary for an A* answer.

societal convention — her father's determination to marry her to a respectable man of position, but someone whom she does not love, was typical behaviour at this time.

When Juliet kills herself this is a quick and rash act but it is also courageous, as she cannot face life without Romeo. Her passionate nature develops as a result of her deep feelings for Romeo. She resists what is expected of a 13-year-old girl of this time and she is determined to be with the man she wants, in life or death, no matter what the consequences.

Mercutio

Shakespeare presents this character as passionate, clever and courageous and with a highly developed sense of honour, as would have been expected from someone of his social standing (remember, he is related to the Prince) and age at this time. We also see that his interest in his friend, Romeo, seems to far outweigh the interest Romeo feels for him. In the scenes where Mercutio appears and is not talking to Romeo, the conversation is led by Mercutio and revolves around his friend: where he is, what he's doing, his emotional or mental state.

Romeo's mind, on the other hand, is almost entirely pre-occupied with first Rosaline and then Juliet. He jokes with Mercutio and enjoys their battles of wit. He is clearly fond of Mercutio, but not to the exclusion of all else. Romeo's response to Mercutio's death shows how deeply he cares for him, but Mercutio's death aside, his first priority is love of a romantic nature, for women.

If we compare the way in which Mercutio speaks of women to the language Shakespeare gives to Romeo, it is easy to understand why many critics have suggested two things about Mercutio: first that he does not like women very much and second that he does not 'like' women very much, as in, he is not physically attracted to them. In all his speeches about women (and remember, most also involve Romeo in one way or another), they are seen as objects of physical lust and 'love' for them is seen as ridiculous and even un-manly. When Romeo disappears after the feast, Mercutio tries to tease him out of hiding with words such as 'madman! passion! lover!', telling him to 'cry but "Ay me"' or 'love' or 'dove', showing that he sees Romeo as having been made effeminate through love of women. When this doesn't work, he taunts him with a

> **Pause for thought**
>
> Mercutio is fond of Romeo and expresses strong opinions against loving women. What might these details suggest to some regarding the exact nature of Mercutio's feelings for Romeo?

Harold Perrineau as Mercutio

Characterisation

graphic description of Rosaline in the act of sex. When Romeo still does not respond, Mercutio concludes somewhat insultingly of Romeo 'The ape is dead', suggesting that Romeo has been made a fool by love and is as good as dead. Romeo's response to this, 'he jests at scars that never felt a wound', confirms to the audience that Mercutio has never been in love.

Mercutio's pre-occupation with his friend is underlined the next time we see him. His first words are:

> Where the dev'l should this Romeo be?
> Came he not home tonight?   (2.4 1–2)

He blames Romeo's absence and his emotional and mental state on Rosaline, calling her a 'hard hearted wench' and saying she will 'make him run mad'. When it comes to the question of whether Romeo is fit to confront Tybalt's challenge, Mercutio says, 'the very pin of his heart [is] cleft with the blind bow-boy's butt-shaft; and is he a man to encounter Tybalt?'

This scorn for women and matters of love is reinforced when Benvolio announces 'here comes Romeo' and Mercutio states, 'Without his roe, like a dried herring. O flesh,/flesh, how art thou fishified!', debasing what he imagines has kept Romeo from him. Although Mercutio knows Romeo and Rosaline will not have consummated their relationship (i.e. had sex) he makes the prospect sound very unappealing. He goes on to speak of women famed for the love their beauty inspired in men, calling 'Dido a dowdy, Cleopatra a gypsy, Helen and Hero/hildings and harlots…'. In Act 3 scene 1 Benvolio, the voice of reason, urges Mercutio to go inside and away from a potential brawl with the Capulets, but Mercutio refuses saying, 'I will not budge for no man's pleasure, I.' Mercutio's agitation is highlighted by the fact that Shakespeare presents his speeches in prose here and not verse, as with his earlier speeches regarding the absence of Romeo. He is highly strung and spoiling for a fight.

Romeo's attempts to pacify Tybalt are met with horror by Mercutio, who (unlike the audience) knows nothing of Romeo's marriage to Tybalt's kinswoman. He sees Romeo's submission as 'vile' and 'dishonourable'. His stepping in at this point could be interpreted in a number of ways. He may here suddenly see Romeo as having been unworthy of his loyalty and love. On the other hand, his sudden intervention may be a means of protecting his friend from further embarrassment and dishonour.

In his dying moments the repetition of 'A plague a' both your houses!' 'your houses!' (3.1 lines 83 and 97) emphasises how he feels it is the families' stupidity that has caused his death.

Pause for thought

Mercutio's opinions on love, women and life in general are certainly different from Romeo's. Consider whether this is his structural role in the play. Is it only when Mercutio dies that Romeo becomes truly swept away in the tragedy?

Grade *booster*

Higher grade answers will note that, like other characters in the play, Mercutio claims no personal responsibility for events. Mercutio may not blame fortune, fate or the stars for his death, but he does blame the Montagues and the Capulets. Is Mercutio's death entirely the result of the feud, or does Shakespeare wish us to consider other possible causes rooted in Mercutio's own character?

Elizabethan and modern audiences would, almost certainly, have enjoyed Mercutio's humorous comments, his bawdy jokes and pun-riddled dialogue, as well as his story telling (Queen Mab), his singing and his rhyming. By having him murdered by Tybalt, half-way through the play, Shakespeare chose to shock and sadden his audience, signalling the beginning of the tragic half of the play.

Benvolio

Benvolio's role is as a peacemaker and a figure of calm common sense throughout the play.

He is a good friend to Romeo and Mercutio and advises both of them to be calm. It is, fittingly, Benvolio who is asked to explain what has happened in Act 3 scene 1. His account is a true reflection of what has happened with no added extra details or lies, showing that Benvolio is a true character and honest, in a world where honesty is often forgotten. This is the last we see of him, as his roles in the play as friend and voice of reason are no longer relevant to the development of the action.

Tybalt

Tybalt, Juliet's cousin, acts aggressively in every scene he appears in. In Act 1 scene 1 he threatens one of the play's most honest characters, Benvolio, with death:

> Turn thee, Benvolio, look upon thy death.   (1.1 58)

We never discover why there is a feud between the families, but it seems that Tybalt enjoys the opportunity to fight. This may be because he is bored and has nothing else to do with his time. It should be noted that young men of his social status did not work for a living as they didn't need to. He also responds to the antagonism of others in Act 1 scene 1 and fights to uphold his honour and that of his family.

When Benvolio discusses Tybalt with Montague he gives an honest assessment of his character, calling him 'fiery' and having 'defiance', and he emphasises how he 'hissed him in scorn' (1.1 100–03).

At Capulet's party in Act 1 scene 5, Tybalt sees Romeo's presence as a challenge to the family honour and an insult. Without Capulet's intervention he may well have reduced the party to a bloodbath. He is so convinced that Romeo is there just to laugh at them that it appears he is paranoid about the Montagues.

Mercutio's description of Tybalt is less forgiving than Benvolio's, calling him 'More than Prince of Cats'. He declares that Tybalt is affected, meaning

---

Key quotation

I do but keep the peace.
(1.1 59)

Key quotation

This is the truth, or let Benvolio die.
(3.1 166)

Pause for thought

Did Shakespeare intend his audience simply to dislike Tybalt, or might he also be seen as a victim of the values of his society?

Key quotation

What, drawn and talk of peace? I hate the word,

As I hate hell, all Montagues, and thee.

Have at thee, coward.
(1.1 61–63)

Characterisation

that he keeps up with the modern styles, and calls him a 'whore' and a 'fashion-monger…'.

Tybalt taunts Mercutio in Act 3 scene 1 implying, in his use of the word 'consort', that Mercutio follows Romeo around like a wife and calling Romeo a 'boy' to irritate him. The value of honour in Elizabethan England and, we assume, Verona at the end of the sixteenth century, means that it is appropriate that Tybalt fights Mercutio when challenged, and when Mercutio is killed Romeo has to gain revenge. There is no great build up to Tybalt's death: he is killed and the story quickly moves on. He does not get a final word which, dramatically speaking, makes the moment of his death less significant than Mercutio's. Shakespeare may be manipulating his audience to feel more sympathy for Mercutio than Tybalt.

Tybalt has an important role in the play as his violent actions result in the death of one of Romeo's best friends and cause Romeo's banishment.

Capulet

Capulet, as head of one of the two rival families in the play, is presented as an authoritative and powerful man. The first time we see Capulet he is desperate to fight in the brawl at the beginning of Act 1.

He enjoys putting on a spectacle and is holding a large party at his house. He acts as the perfect host, chastising Tybalt for wanting to create chaos at the party. His constant desire for authority is emphasised by his comment to Tybalt: 'Am I the master here, or you?' (1.5 77).

Capulet shows his aggressive, almost cruel nature in Act 3 scene 5 when he threatens to throw Juliet out of his house if she refuses to marry Paris. In the context of the play and Elizabethan England, however, the father, as head of a household, did not expect to be disagreed with and his word was law, which explains his reaction to Juliet's disobedience.

The attitude of Capulet towards Juliet's marriage changes completely between the start of the play and the scene where he commands Juliet to marry Paris. The initial comments he makes — such as 'let two more summers whither in their pride/ere we may think her ripe to be a bride' (1.2 10–11), that mothers so early made 'are too soon marr'd' (1.2 13), and 'My will to her consent is but a part…' (1.2 17) — all attest to his wish to give Juliet time to allow her to make her own choice in matrimony. The fact that he changes his attitude, after the murder of Tybalt, raises many interesting questions. Capulet complains to his wife in Juliet's presence:

> …Day, night, work, play,
> Alone, in company, still my care hath been
> To have her matched;…   (3.5 176–78)

Key quotation

… old Capulet, and Montague,

Have thrice disturbed the quiet of our streets

(1.1 81–82)

This suggests that he sees the match as the height of what any young girl could possibly want and is truly hurt that she is ungrateful for all his efforts on her behalf. It should be noted that Shakespeare does offer some exoneration for Capulet's sudden change of plans for Juliet, as Lady Capulet says to Juliet:

> Well, well, thou hast a careful father, child,
> One who, to put thee from thy heaviness,
> Hath sorted out a sudden day of joy   (3.5 107–09)

Later, the idea that Capulet has brought the wedding plans forward to cheer Juliet up from what he believes to be mourning for Tybalt, is confirmed by Paris's words to the Friar:

> …her father counts it dangerous
> That she do give her sorrow so much sway;
> And in his wisdom hastes our marriage
> To stop the inundation of her tears   (4.1 9–12)

However, we must also remember that his family have just been blamed for the death of a kinsman of the Prince (Mercutio), so marrying his daughter to 'a man of wax', highly reputed throughout Verona, at this particular juncture, would do his family honour no harm at all, and this could explain his change of outlook.

Pause for thought

What do Capulet's words to Juliet — '…I'll not be forsworn' — reveal to the audience about what is most important to him?

Grade *booster*

Watch the Luhrmann and Zeffirelli films and note the ways in which they hint at an affair between Lady Capulet and Tybalt. For higher grades you will need to explore the ways in which this suggestion is created. Look at camera work, use of music and re-allocation of lines from Lord Capulet to Lady Capulet.

Lady Capulet

Lady Capulet, Juliet's mother, appears to be a typical female character of this period. She seems dominated by her husband, with whom she has a distant and formal relationship and while she appears loyal to him on the surface, we never see any signs of affection or love between them. She also has a fairly distant relationship with her daughter but enjoys the luxuries her wealthy lifestyle gives her. She is determined to see her young daughter married to a man of high status in society, and beyond this she does not question. She reflects the marital conventions of the time, asking Juliet, 'How stands your dispositions to be married?' When Juliet says that it's not something she's thought about, Lady Capulet informs her that it's high time she did as she herself was not only married, but had also given birth to Juliet by her age.

Her rather emotionally charged speech upon the death of Tybalt, her demand of the Prince 'For blood of ours, shed blood of Montague' (3.1 140), and her speech in private to Juliet telling of her plans to murder Romeo have led many modern producers to suggest an illicit affair between Lady

Characterisation

Capulet and Tybalt. (This is shown in various ways in both the Luhrmann and the Zeffirelli productions.)

In Act 3 scene 4 Capulet instructs his wife to go and see Juliet and tell her about Paris's love for her. There is a formality about the way he speaks to her, emphasising her subservience and that their relationship is not necessarily a close one.

When Juliet refuses to marry Paris and asks for her mother to help her, Lady Capulet refuses. This could be interpreted in a number of ways. She might be afraid to tell her husband of her daughter's disobedience, fearing his extreme reaction against herself as being responsible for Juliet's attitude. Lady Capulet may also be seen as resentful of her daughter's strength of character in being able to oppose male dominance in a way that she did not have the strength to. However we read her character here, her inability to do anything practical to help her daughter is clear; in this society, men hold all the cards. Lady Capulet sees Juliet as not being free to make her own decisions and feels she must accept, just as she has, the code of practice developed by the men of Renaissance society.

Paris

Paris is a good-looking, wealthy young man who wants to marry Juliet. He sees nothing unusual about his wish to marry a girl who is not yet 14 and points out that many 'younger than she are happy mothers made'. When he calls Juliet 'his lady' and 'wife' before he has married her, this is a reflection of the degree to which women were meant to fall in line with the wishes of men. Clearly, Paris sees himself as a bit of a catch and does not expect any resistance from Juliet.

When he thinks that Juliet is dead, Paris appears devastated. He is shown to be, by the standards of the time, both honourable and brave in his willingness to protect her final resting place from the insult he imagines Romeo has come to commit. The speech Shakespeare gives to Romeo shows that even he sees Paris as a victim of circumstances, and not personally to blame for the tragedy. Here, Paris is also allowed some dying words, unlike Tybalt, showing Paris in a positive light. Shakespeare even has Romeo agreeing to lay Paris beside the woman they both loved, showing the degree to which he respects Paris, when he could well have despised him, seeing him as the man who had caused Juliet's death.

> **Key quotation**
>
> Wife, go you to her ere you go to bed;
>
> Acquaint her here of my son Paris' love,
>
> (3.4 15–16)

> **Pause for thought**
>
> Consider how Luhrmann and Zeffirelli's interpretations of Lady Capulet's hypocrisy are reinforced by the response of the Nurse to Juliet's predicament in being forced to marry Paris.

> **Pause for thought**
>
> Why is Paris described by the Nurse as being 'a man of wax' (1.3 77)?
>
> What possible interpretations might this bear?
>
> Why does Paris try to ignore Juliet's less than adoring responses? If you were Paris and had any indication that Juliet did not love you would you just give up? (Remember his earlier discussion with Capulet in Act 1 scene 2.)

> **Key quotation**
>
> ...O give me thy hand,
> One writ with me in sour misfortune's book!
> I'll bury thee in a triumphant grave.   (5.3 81–83)

Prince

> **Key quotation**
>
> Three civil brawls, bred of an airy word
>
> By thee, old Capulet, and Montague,
>
> Have thrice disturbed the quiet of our streets
>
> (1.1 80–82)

The Prince decides the laws and acts as judge and jury when deciding how justice is to be carried out. This form of justice may have been more common at the time of the play, but is different from today. He arrives in Act 1 scene 1 to take control and calm the fight between the feuding families.

He is also used by Shakespeare in Act 1 scene 1 as a device to tell the audience what has been happening. He threatens death if the families brawl again, showing his power and authority.

In Act 3 scene 1 he banishes Romeo rather than sentencing him to death — he agrees that Romeo's actions were wrong but can also understand the reasons for those actions. He also reveals that Mercutio is related to him and thus his own blood 'lies a-bleeding' as a result of this brawl. This shows a merciful and sensible side to his character.

> **Pause for thought**
>
> What does the fact that the Prince has let the families off twice before suggest about his methods of rule?
>
> Why has Shakespeare chosen to call him Escalus?

Shakespeare gives the Prince, the character of highest rank, the last words of the play. This both follows the literary convention of the time, and also uses the Prince's voice to underline a moral message. The Prince states that Heaven has found ways of punishing them all, including himself who, for 'winking at' (turning a blind eye to) the families' 'discords', has suffered the loss of relations.

Nurse

> **Grade booster**
>
> To gain a higher mark it is useful to explore the role of the Nurse in detail. If she had refused to help Juliet and Romeo, the tragedy may not have occurred. Does she ever accept any responsibility for the tragic 'death' of her 'young lady'?

The Nurse acts as the protector and helper of Juliet and seems far closer, emotionally, to Juliet than her mother is. She is often a comic character and her speeches are full of sexual innuendo, for example when she tells the bawdy story of Juliet falling on her front as a child and her husband's comment that when she is older she'll fall backwards (i.e. have sex). This interest in sexual matters is reflected in the eagerness with which the Nurse is complicit in arranging what she knows to be a marriage that Juliet's parents would never allow to happen. This reveals her as irresponsible and a little childish.

After Juliet has married Romeo and after the death of Tybalt, the Nurse continues to help Juliet as much as she can, showing that she does wish Juliet to be happy. In Act 3 scene 2 she offers Juliet hope by saying that she knows where Romeo is and will bring him to her to give her comfort. She also warns Juliet of her mother's approach when Juliet is with Romeo and leaps to her defence when Capulet is enraged with her on her refusal to marry Paris.

> **Key quotation**
>
> I am the drudge and toil in your delight;
>
> But you shall bear the burden soon at night.
>
> (2.5 74–75)

However, even the Nurse draws the line at outright defiance of Lord Capulet's commands, saying 'I think you had better marry with the County'.

Characterisation

She tries to reconcile Juliet to the arrangement by telling her that Paris is by far the better match, Romeo being 'a dishclout' (a dish cloth) by comparison.

Shakespeare shows her to be totally unabashed in suggesting that Juliet coolly transfer her affections to Paris, fresh from the embrace of her newly married husband. For the Nurse, the critical factor is that Juliet will not be found out, telling her, '…here it is:/Romeo is banished…/…he dares ne'er come back to challenge you' (3.5 212–14). This shows that male oppression has led her to feel no guilt at all in using deceit to cover her tracks and that she sees relationships with the opposite sex in utterly shallow terms. To her, one man is as good as another provided they are good looking and have lots of money. The fact that Paris is better looking and wealthier than Romeo makes him the more desirable match in the Nurse's eyes.

> **Pause for thought**
>
> The Nurse is perfectly happy for Juliet to marry Paris. What does this say about attitudes towards marriage typical of this period? What point might Shakespeare be making here, through the Nurse's casual acceptance of Juliet's sudden second match?

Montague and Lady Montague

We see the Montagues, the rival family to the Capulets, few times in the play. Lady Montague tries to prevent her husband from joining the fight in Act 1 scene 1 and declares how she is glad her son Romeo was not at the fight, showing the protective nature of her love for him. She also asks Benvolio to try to find out what is ailing Romeo, again showing her concern for him.

The depth of her love for Romeo is further highlighted when Montague arrives in the final scene and reveals that his wife has died of a broken heart after the banishment of Romeo.

That Romeo chooses to confide in the Priest rather than his father is not really any surprise. His disgust at the feud caused by the male heads of the two families is clear when he asks Benvolio what the 'fray' at the start of the play was about, but then quickly adds, 'Yet tell me not…for I have heard it all.' That he chooses not to confide in his mother is more interesting and is probably a result of this just not being the done thing at this time. However, Romeo is clearly a lover of women and this at least hints at a loving relationship with his mother. Remember, Juliet is not the only woman who loves Romeo even unto death in this play.

> *Key quotation*
>
> **Right glad I am he was not at this fray.**
> (1.1 108)

> *Key quotation*
>
> **Alas, my liege, my wife is dead tonight;**
>
> **Grief of my son's exile hath stopp'd her breath.**
> (5.3 210–11)

Friar Lawrence

Friar Lawrence's role as a man with knowledge of drugs, medicines and potions is established from the outset in the lines:

> O mickle is the powerful grace that lies
> In herbs, plants, stones, and their true qualities: (2.3 15–16)

Here he muses over the power of herbs to do both good and bad, perhaps linking to the Friar's own power to influence events. Romeo calls him

> **Pause for thought**
>
> The Friar has a low opinion of Romeo's feelings for Juliet and only helps him in order to promote peace between the families. What does this tell us about the Friar's opinion regarding love in marriage? Does he behave in a responsible manner by agreeing to marry Romeo and Juliet so suddenly when he has just urged a calm and careful approach?

'my ghostly father' (2.3 45) and 'ghostly sire' (2.2 188), adding a sense of mystery and authority to his character, reinforced by the fact that he is often alone and tries to keep out of the public eye.

When Romeo asks the Friar to marry him to Juliet the Friar can be forgiven for thinking Romeo is too rash and hasty with his love. He urges Romeo to be more calm and less hasty, upbraiding him for his fickle nature:

> Lo here upon thy cheek the stain doth sit
> Of an old tear that is not washed off yet.
>
> (2.3 75–76)

He is truly angered at Romeo's rapid change of affections, stating that 'Young men's love then lies/Not truly in their hearts, but in their eyes' (2.3 67–68). Yet he agrees to help Romeo because he hopes the feud between the two families will end as a result of their love.

The Friar, like Romeo, has a tendency to blame events on outside forces and does not anywhere accept responsibility for things going wrong.

> **Grade booster**
>
> Higher band candidates will explore the complex nature of the Friar's character. As with all of Shakespeare's characters, he is more than one-dimensional and he has his good points and his failings. He may be a priest, but he is also portrayed as very human. What are his good points and what are his failings?

> **Key quotation**
>
> Wisely and slow. They stumble that run fast.

The Friar is someone whom people in the play rely upon for advice, and yet it is debatably because of the Friar's advice that Romeo, Paris, Juliet and Lady Montague all end up dead. Seeing Romeo and Paris dead, he curses time and fate that have allowed this to happen:

> …Ah, what an unkind hour
> Is guilty of this lamentable chance!
>
> (5.3 145–46)

> **Pause for thought**
>
> The Friar blames 'lamentable chance' for Romeo's death. Does Shakespeare simply want the audience to accept the Friar's apportioning of blame here?

The Friar's role at the end of the play is to summarise events for the Prince, and for the audience too in case they have missed anything in the noisy Elizabethan theatre. He states at the end that 'if ought in this/Miscarried by my fault, let my old life/Be sacrificed…' suggesting that he is willing to die if he has been in any way at fault. What is left open to debate is whether or not he thinks he is in any way to blame. The word 'if' in the quotation above is important.

Characterisation

Grade *focus*

Questions may ask you to look at one character and to comment on their role in the play. You may be asked:

Is Romeo rash, passionate and impetuous in the play?

or:

What role does the Nurse have in *Romeo and Juliet*?

For more details see the *Sample essays* section on p. 81.

Grades G–D

In this range of grades, candidates' answers are likely to deal with the characters as real people only. There might well be detailed accounts of the actions of Romeo and Juliet and comments about their love for each other. At this level candidates will not tend to discuss the way in which the characters are created to help Shakespeare illustrate his themes.

The better candidates in this grade range will support comments with references to the text.

Grades C–A*

In this grade range, examiners will expect to see that you know about the actions of the characters (as above), but also that you realise that aspects of general human behaviour can be seen through the main characters. The best candidates will be equally able to discuss the characters as psychologically realistic creations to help the writer illustrate and explore his themes.

Review your learning

(Answers are given on p. 93.)

1. Select three quotations that illustrate the major character aspects of Romeo, Juliet, Mercutio and Tybalt.
2. What sort of a character is Romeo?
3. What sort of a character is Juliet?
4. Comment on the ways in which Romeo, Juliet, Friar Lawrence and the Nurse change during the course of the play.
5. Discuss the relationships between:
    a Romeo and Juliet
    b The Capulets and the Montagues
    c Juliet and the Nurse
    d Romeo and Friar Lawrence
    e Romeo and Tybalt

More interactive questions and answers online.

Style

- What features does the term 'style' refer to?
- Is *Romeo and Juliet* a tragedy?
- What use does Shakespeare make of verse and prose?
- How does Shakespeare use imagery and symbolism?
- What other devices are used?

When you write about style, you are showing that you understand an important fact: the playwright has numerous choices. Your job as a literary critic — because that's what you really are when you write your exam essay — is to identify what choices Shakespeare has made and to assess how effective they are. Shakespeare has made choices about all of the following stylistic features:

- dialogue (conversation) — how it is used and how realistic it is
- imagery — the way in which the writer uses word pictures
- symbolism
- verse and prose
- irony

> **Grade booster**
>
> Commenting on and exploring how Shakespeare juxtaposes tragic and comic scenes (puts them alongside one another) to highlight the idea of chaos will gain you a higher mark.

Tragedy and comedy

Romeo and Juliet is neither tragedy nor comedy. It is a mixture of both, which makes it a tragic comedy. There are a number of moments in the play that are funny, followed by scenes of violence or tragedy. This begins in Act 1 scene 1 when the jovial, if slightly threatening comments of Sampson and Gregory develop into a deadly street brawl. Romeo and Mercutio joke together not long before Tybalt arrives in Act 3, the scene ending in Mercutio's tragic death.

The Chorus

The Chorus is a device common in Greek tragedy. A group of speakers, often made up of minor characters from the play, address the audience directly, acting as a bridge between the actors on the stage, who are oblivious to the audience, and the audience themselves. It is a clever device, allowing insights into the minds and hearts of the characters and is often used to offer philosophical or moral commentary on their behaviour to provoke thought in the audience. The Chorus operates in a similar way to a third-person narrative voice in a novel, where an omniscient (all powerful, all seeing) voice can see precisely what is motivating the characters that are under discussion.

The Prologue

The Prologue, spoken by the Chorus at the start of the play, is a kind of foreword and is written in **sonnet form**. Each of the three **quatrains** (set of four lines) provides a succinct opportunity to sum up an important aspect of the story:

- **First quatrain:** two families of equally high standing in Verona have had a quarrel for many years and now it will erupt afresh and much blood will be shed.
- **Second quatrain:** a child is born to each family, the children fall in love and their deaths end the quarrel.
- **Third quatrain:** how all of this happens, their love, their parents' anger and finally the end of the quarrel, is the business of the play which will take about two hours.

The final two lines, a **rhyming couplet**, neatly emphasise an important point: the noise levels common in the Elizabethan theatre would have made it difficult for many in the audience to hear the dialogue of the play, hence the suggestion that if they 'with patient ears attend/What ***here*** shall miss, [the actors'] toil shall strive to mend'. The **pun** on the word 'here', suggests that if they cannot *hear* the storyline from the Prologue, they should be able to understand what is going on from watching the action of the play carefully.

Act 2

We see the Chorus providing commentary on the characters at the start of Act 2:

> That fair for which love groaned for and would die,
> With tender Juliet matched is now not fair.
> Now Romeo is beloved, and loves again,
> Alike bewitchèd by the charm of looks;

Shakespeare is clearly using the Chorus to ensure that his audience pick up the point (if they don't hear it elsewhere) that Romeo's 'love' for women is driven by the way in which they look. Not only this, the words 'That fair for which loved groaned for and would die' refer not to Romeo's willingness to die for Juliet, but for Rosaline. That Romeo is a young man whose love lies in his eyes not in his heart, has been played out effectively in the previous scene where he has forgotten all about Rosaline, saying he has never seen 'true beauty until this night'. The idea is also reinforced through the Friar's words, 'young men's love lies then […] in their eyes'; and in Romeo's own dismissal of Rosaline when he tells the Friar, 'I have forgot that name and that name's woe'.

We may have heard Shakespeare's point about Romeo's character before this point, but the Chorus's statements are significant. The voice of the Chorus members traditionally carries more weight by virtue of the fact that they are objective, standing outside the central action of the play. We can take their words as truth. Through the Chorus, Shakespeare tells us that it is Romeo and Juliet's 'passion' that will lend them power to overcome the obstacles in their way.

Prose and poetry

The language used in Shakespeare's plays is not the sort of language you hear today.

There were certain theatrical conventions that Shakespeare followed when writing his plays. The characters speak using either poetry (verse) or prose (normal speech). Characters lower in rank speak mostly in prose, for example servants such as Sampson and Gregory in Act 1 scene 1, the serving men in Act 1 scene 5 and the musicians in Act 4 scene 5. Characters higher in rank, such as the Prince, Capulet, Romeo and Juliet, speak in verse. This makes these characters sound more important and poetic.

It should be noted, however, that in certain scenes, Mercutio most notably speaks not in verse but in prose and this may be done to stress his disturbed state of mind when he is fretting about Romeo.

All the lines are the same length and contain about **ten syllables**. In his verse, Shakespeare uses **iambic pentameter** which consists of five soft beats and five hard beats. For instance:

    - / - / - / - / - /
    But, soft! what light through yonder window breaks?

Each hard beat is followed immediately by a soft beat. The actors would not speak emphasising the hard and soft beats as this would sound silly, but this was the conventional writing style of this period.

Sub-plot and comic relief

Most of Shakespeare's plays have sub-plots, which involve other characters in a secondary plot that is related to the main one. There is no such sub-plot in *Romeo and Juliet* and either one or both of the main characters are on stage for most of the play. The brief interludes with the servants in Act 1 scenes 1 and 5 and the musicians in Act 4 scene 4 serve to break up the intense focus on the main characters' brief relationship, allowing for some **comic relief**.

This sort of **juxtapositioning** (placing alongside one another) of comic and serious scenes is common to tragedies of this period and offers 'relief' to the audience from the serious and tragic elements of the play. It is important to note, though, that the comic scenes do normally reflect the serious themes of the play. For example, the humorous sexual innuendos of Sampson and Gregory at the start of the play mirror in a comic fashion the serious treatment of the passionate, sexual drive behind 'love' that we see explored through the other characters. This is reflected not only in the passion between Romeo and Juliet, but in the attitudes of characters such as Benvolio, Mercutio and the Friar towards Romeo's passionate nature, and of the Nurse, Lady Capulet and Lord Capulet towards Juliet's relationships with men.

In exactly the same way, the thumb-biting incident is a reflection of just how petty the original cause of the feud is, highlighted in the next, serious scene where the Prince tells us the feud has been caused, or 'bred', of careless and petty words issuing from both Capulet and Montague. Shakespeare uses the lower characters to parody the concerns of the higher characters in the play. This, again, was a common literary device of the times and one with which any Elizabethan audience would have been familiar.

(For more detailed analysis of the structure of the play, read the section on *Plot and structure*.)

Language

Crude language and puns

The crude language used in the play would have been seen as a huge source of humour for the audience watching the play. Actors would certainly have exaggerated the rude jokes to gain maximum impact in front of a rowdy audience.

The many sexual **innuendos** and **puns** (words with more than one meaning) create a comic ambiguity, flattering the intelligence of the audience and inviting them to laugh. For example, the double meaning of Gregory's line, 'draw thy tool…' (1.1 28), and Sampson's response, 'my naked weapon is out', takes little imagination to work out. Some of Mercutio's double entendres are slightly more difficult to interpret, but all of them make sex between men and women sound a pretty bestial affair and do not have much to do with Romeo's romantic notions of 'love'.

Mercutio's bawdy dialogue with the Nurse provides comic relief

Text focus

Consider the significance of Mercutio's words to Benvolio in Act 2 scene 1, which he hopes that the hidden Romeo will hear. Benvolio has told Mercutio that his taunts about Rosaline will anger Romeo, and Mercutio responds:

> 'This cannot anger him; 'twould anger him
> To raise a spirit in his mistress' circle,
> Of some strange nature, letting it there stand
> Till she had laid it and conjured it down:'   (2.1 23–26)

This innuendo about male erections and where they are placed would have not only been clear but hilarious to an Elizabethan audience. The imagery continues with a clear vision of Rosaline 'letting' these erections 'stand' in 'her circle' until she 'conjure(s)' them down, Mercutio's design being specifically to goad Romeo out of his hiding by suggesting graphic images of Rosaline having sex with other men. However, the **irony** is that while it might have had exactly that effect a few hours earlier, since Romeo no longer cares about Rosaline, his words miss the mark entirely.

Pause for thought

Work out the meaning of some of the crude words and phrases from Act 1 scene 1.
- 'A dog of that house shall move me to stand' (line 10)
- 'I will take the wall of any man or maid of Montague's' (lines 10–11)
- 'I will be civil with the maids; I will cut off their heads.' (lines 19–20)
- 'Me they shall feel while I am able to stand…' (line 25)
- 'my naked weapon is out…' (line 29)

Style

Don't be fooled into thinking that this sort of humour is included by Shakespeare merely to win cheap laughs. Rather, the humour reveals something about his themes. Here, we are invited to explore different attitudes towards 'love'. The crude and bawdy language of love is contrasted with the highly poetic language of love used by Romeo and Juliet. In spite of the high nature of their language, their love still appears to be founded upon physical attraction (see *Plot and structure, Characterisation, Themes*).

Oxymorons

Shakespeare uses many oxymorons in the play. An oxymoron is a phrase that contains two contradictory words. The effect is often to show conflict in feelings.

When Juliet says good night to Romeo at the end of Act 2 scene 2, she thinks that their 'parting' is 'sweet' in that they will be soon together again, but she is still sorry as she does not want to be apart from him:

> Good night, good night! Parting is such sweet sorrow… (2.2 184)

> ### Text focus
>
> In Act 3 scene 2, Juliet's response to the news of Romeo's killing of Tybalt is a list of oxymorons:
>
> 'A damnèd saint, an honourable villain!
> O nature, what hadst thou to do in hell,
> When thou didst bower the spirit of a fiend
> In mortal paradise of such sweet flesh?
> Was ever book containing such vile matter
> So fairly bound? O that deceit should dwell
> In such a gorgeous palace!' (3.2 79–85)
>
> What opposing ideas are introduced here and how do they reveal Juliet's feelings for Romeo at this point?

Rhyming couplets

Many of the scenes in *Romeo and Juliet* end with rhyming couplets, a technique Shakespeare often used to signal the end of a phase of action. Note that the original performances of his plays were not divided into the 'five acts containing several scenes' formula that we see today. Juliet finishes Act 2 scene 2 with a rhyming couplet to indicate that this really is the end of the encounter. Notice how Romeo also ends this same scene with rhyming couplets:

> Sleep dwell upon thine eyes, peace in thy breast!
> Would I were sleep and peace, so sweet to rest!
> Hence will I to my ghostly sire's close cell,
> His help to crave, and my dear hap to tell. (2.2 186–89)

Rhyming couplets are also used to emphasise important points or moments in the play. Rhyme works as a memory aid and often the words with the most important meanings are those that rhyme at the end of the lines. In this way, Shakespeare ensures that his meaning has some impact on his audience. For example, the Prince ends the play with a rhyming couplet:

> For never was a story of more woe
> Than this of Juliet and her Romeo. (5.3 309–10)

Repetition

There are many examples of repetition in the play, a tactic used to emphasise certain feelings and ideas. Juliet repeats Romeo's name several times in Act 2 scene 2:

> O Romeo, Romeo, wherefore art thou Romeo? (2.2 33)

The constant repetition of 'name' in her following speech (lines 38–49) shows how aggrieved she feels that Romeo is a Montague, and therefore a great enemy of her family.

In Act 4 scene 5 the repetition of 'look', 'O me!' and 'help!' shows the desperation in both Lady Capulet and the Nurse's reactions to Juliet's death, showing how much she means to her family.

Imagery

> **Grade booster**
>
> To improve your writing you should explore examples of metaphors and other linguistic techniques. Give an example, explain the technique being used and explore the effect of the image on shaping the meaning we take from it.

The term 'imagery' refers to the kind of word pictures a writer creates to help us imagine what is being described. There are three main kinds of imagery used in *Romeo and Juliet*:

- **simile** — when one thing is compared with another, using 'like' or 'as'
- **metaphor** — when something is described as if it actually is something else
- **personification** — when something that is not human is given human characteristics

Shakespeare uses these kinds of imagery throughout the play.

Metaphors

There are numerous metaphors for love throughout the play. In Act 1 scene 1, Romeo compares love to 'a fire sparkling in lovers' eyes' (line 182) — as it is similar to a fire, sparking powerful, heated emotions. In the same speech he also describes love as 'Being vexed, a sea nourished with loving tears' (line 183) — as the vast number of tears shed by lovers who are sad or angry ('vexed') is comparable to a sea.

> **Pause for thought**
>
> What other qualities are given to love by the following examples from the same speech?
>
> '...a madness most discreet,
> A choking gall and a preserving sweet.' (1.1 184–85)

Personification

The Friar, in his first appearance, personifies day and night as day being someone

Style

happy and smiling at the bad tempered night. Day was traditionally seen, at this time, as a positive time and night as a dark, mysterious time:

> The grey-eyed morn smiles on the frowning night (2.3 1)

In Act 2 scene 2 Romeo tells Juliet he has found her bedroom because the figure of 'love' told him where it was. He talks of love as if it were a friend telling him where to find her:

> JULIET: By whose direction found'st thou out this place?
> ROMEO: By Love, that first did prompt me to inquire;
> He lent me counsel, and I lent him eyes. (2.2 79–81)

Disease imagery

Many of Shakespeare's plays are rich in disease imagery and *Romeo and Juliet* is no exception. In Act 1 scene 1 Romeo says he feels diseased and 'sick' because he has been rejected by Rosaline. He feels so 'ill' he needs to make a will in case he dies, yet he still has the wit to point out how the word 'ill' sounds similar to 'will', which makes him feel worse:

> Bid a sick man in sadness make his will —
> A word ill urged to one that is so ill (1.1 193–94)

The idea of sickness is also juxtaposed against the beauty of Juliet. Romeo compares her to the 'fair sun', something that gives light and life, and contrasts her with the envious moon (which looks 'pale' and unwell).

Benvolio tells Romeo that love is like an eye infection and the only way for the poison of the old infection (his love for Rosaline) to 'die' (be cured) is to get a new infection, a new love. Using the word 'infection' implies that even with a new love, he will still be diseased, showing what Benvolio considers to be the danger of love:

> Take thou some new infection to thy eye,
> And the rank poison of the old will die. (1.2 48–49)

When the Prince berates Capulet and Montague for their 'civil brawls', he describes their hands as 'cankered' (1.1 85–86), which means diseased.

> **Key quotation**
>
> Arise, fair sun, and kill the envious moon,
>
> Who is already sick and pale with grief
> (2.2 4–5)

Religious imagery

The play is full of imagery that links religion with love. When Romeo and Juliet meet for the first time they describe the act of kissing as saintly. Romeo begins the imagery of 'pilgrims' and 'holy shrines', elevating the nature of his love for Juliet to the status of a pure and holy thing:

> Have not saints lips, and holy palmers too? (1.5 100)

Lips are used both for kissing and for praying. Romeo describes their first kiss as like a prayer, saying that kissing Juliet feels as if her pure lips have taken away all his sins:

> Then move not, while my prayer's effect I take.
> Thus from my lips, by yours, my sin is purged. (1.5 105–06)

> **Key quotation**
>
> Good pilgrim, you do wrong your hand too much,
>
> Which mannerly devotion shows in this,
>
> For saints have hands that pilgrims' hands do touch,
>
> And palm to palm is holy palmers' kiss.
>
> (1.5 96–99)

Depending on how the scene is played, this could be romantic, or there could be hints of humour in a young man's less than naive attempts to seduce a seemingly innocent girl. However, we have already seen the passionate and earnest nature of Romeo when believing himself in love. What we might question here is not whether he is genuine or not, but just how deeply his love goes given that he can transfer it so rapidly and that it seems to rest purely on 'looks', as is later pointed out by the Chorus and the Friar. Juliet's comment 'You kiss by the book' (1.5 109) could be a reference to the Bible, further linking the act of kissing Romeo to something holy and religious.

Imagery surrounding Juliet

There is much imagery throughout the play dealing with the beauty and gloriousness of Juliet. She is compared to the sun, giving her the qualities of warmth, of radiant light and of something that gives life and is necessary to survive.

> **Key quotation**
>
> It is the east, and Juliet is the sun.
>
> (2.2 3)

She is also compared, by Romeo, to the stars, when he says her cheeks are so bright they make the stars ashamed, being less bright:

> The brightness of her cheek would shame those stars,
> As daylight doth a lamp; her eyes in heaven
> Would through the airy region stream so bright
> That birds would sing and think it were not night. (2.2 19–22)

All those who speak of Juliet do so in a positive manner, whether it is her father, the Nurse, Romeo or Paris. It is only when Juliet disobeys her father's instructions to marry Paris that we hear anything negative:

> Out, you green-sickness carrion! out, you baggage!
> You tallow-face! (3.5 156–57)

It is more shocking to hear such negative insults being thrown at Juliet when all we have heard, up to this point, are positive words.

Fire imagery

Fire is often associated with passion in love — the image of 'flames of passion' is common even in modern English. Benvolio tells Romeo that

Style

one fire (his old love) can be burnt out by another one, if he finds a new love:

> ...one fire burns out another's burning,
> One pain is lessened by another's anguish; (1.2 44–45)

The image is continued by Romeo who connects fire and love with burning heretics (those who speak up against the church) at the stake. This is **ironic**, as the moment he looks at Juliet with his 'heretic' eyes he falls in love, forgetting about Rosaline and his previous passionate avowals:

> When the devout religion of mine eye
> Maintains such falsehood, then turn tears to fires;
> And these who, often drowned, could never die,
> Transparent heretics, be burnt for liars. (1.2 88–91)

Images of light and darkness

Dark and light are frequently contrasted throughout the play. The lightness of love is covered by the darkness of night (which can link to the theme of disguise). Romeo and Juliet can only declare their love for each other at night when they are hidden from everyone else:

> But that thou overheard'st, ere I was ware,
> My true love's passion: therefore pardon me,
> And not impute this yielding to light love,
> Which the dark night hath so discovered. (2.2 103–06)

The first time Romeo sees Juliet he compares her to the light of burning torches. And he continues to link her to the bright warmth of 'the sun' (2.2 3) and the light of a 'bright angel' (2.2 26).

Images of light are also used in a negative way, however. For example, when Juliet tells Romeo that she feels their 'contract' is too 'rash', she compares it to lightning which disappears before one can finish saying 'it lightens'. This idea of metaphorical darkness stemming from light also appears when the dawn heralds Romeo's departure from Verona. It is at this point that darkness begins to dominate the play. Juliet tries to convince Romeo that the light is a meteor in a desperate bid to keep him there longer:

> Yond light is not daylight, I know it, I:
> It is some meteor that the sun exhaled (3.5 12–13)

This focus on light is contrasted when Juliet thinks of the darkness of the vault where she will lie asleep in Act 4 scene 3. Darkness is also present when the Prince sums up the final mood in Act 5 scene 3:

> **Key quotation**
>
> O she doth teach the torches to burn bright!
> (1.5 43)

> A glooming peace this morning with it brings,
> The sun for sorrow will not show his head.   (5.3 305–06)

Darkness and light can also be related to the idea of good and evil. This is reflected most clearly in the goodness of Romeo and Juliet's love being contrasted with the evil of the feud and the violence underpinning anything connected to the two family's rivalries.

Symbolism

A **symbol** is something that the playwright uses consistently to represent or 'stand for' something else. There is also rather more room for personal interpretation here: not all critics interpret a symbol in exactly the same way.

Bird symbolism

In augury (forecasting the future from signs in nature) birds were seen as extremely important and Shakespeare often uses symbols of birds to illustrate his points. This perhaps also reflects the superstitious nature of his society at the time.

One example is when Benvolio tries to cheer Romeo up in Act 1 scene 2, telling him: 'I will make thee think thy swan a crow' (line 87). He means that the girls at the Capulets' party will make Rosaline, who Romeo thinks is like a beautiful and graceful swan, seem like an ugly crow. It is also significant that the crow was a bird thought to foreshadow death. This is of course **ironic**, in that it is Romeo's love for Juliet, the 'swan', that leads to his death and not his love for Rosaline.

Later, Romeo tells Juliet 'I would I were thy bird' (2.2 182). Juliet develops this image, saying she would look after him so much that she would kill him: 'Yet I should kill thee with much cherishing.' (2.2 183). The **irony** of Romeo's love for Juliet leading to both their deaths is further illustrated in Shakespeare's use of language here.

The lark, a bird of the dawn, is seen as a bad thing as it heralds the separation of the lovers. Normally it would be a good sign, as night ending and light returning was normally seen as a positive event.

> *Key quotation*
>
> Some say the lark makes sweet division;
>
> This doth not so, for she divideth us.
>
> (3.5 29–30)

Irony

Irony is used throughout the play and is one of Shakespeare's favourite devices. **Dramatic irony** is created whenever the audience is aware of something that the players on the stage aren't aware of, so we are one step ahead of them. For example, it is ironic that Juliet responds to Paris greeting her as his 'wife' with the words 'that may be sir, when I may be a wife'. Paris thinks she means that he may call her wife when they are actually married, but we know her to mean that she can't be his wife as she is already married to another man. There are dozens of such examples littered throughout *Romeo and Juliet* and many of them have been highlighted in the various sections of this guide, so keep a look out for them.

Grade *focus*

A* candidates:
- explore and analyse uses of language, offering sophisticated interpretations of authorial intention
- support their comments with an excellent range of imaginatively selected textual detail, saying how these examples affect the overall meaning of the play
- offer a sophisticated analysis of ways in which the structuring of the play also affects audience interpretation

C-grade candidates:
- show a clear understanding of the writer's ideas
- include appropriate textual support to illustrate ideas
- show a clear understanding of some features of language and structure

Grade *booster*

Merely mentioning that Shakespeare uses any of these devices will not gain you a good mark. What you must do is show the examiner that you understand *how* the device works. In other words, how does it achieve Shakespeare's desired effect on the audience?

Review your learning

(Answers are given on p. 93.)

1. Which characters in the play speak in prose and which in poetry, and why?
2. Pick out one example of an oxymoron and explain its effect.
3. Select an example of a metaphor for love and explain its effect.

More interactive questions and answers online.

Themes

- What is a theme?
- What are the main themes in *Romeo and Juliet*?
- How do these themes relate to each other?
- How do these themes relate to the characters?

A **theme** is an idea that the playwright explores. There is no absolutely correct way to define the themes in any text, and in any interpretation of literary themes there is bound to be some overlap.

These are some of the themes of *Romeo and Juliet*:

- love and marriage
- fate, fortune, responsibility
- families and conflict
- friendship and enemies

Love and marriage

Arguably the most important theme of the play is that of love and marriage and the complexities of love. The play is full of images of love:

> Love is a smoke raised with the fume of sighs,
> Being purged, a fire sparkling in lovers' eyes   (1.1 181–82)

> **Key quotation**
>
> Is love a tender thing? it is too rough,
>
> Too rude, too boist'rous, and it pricks like thorn.
>
> (1.4 25–26)

Love causes many of the problems in the play. Romeo is depressed at the start because his love is not returned by Rosaline. Love can be physical and Romeo is unhappy that Rosaline wants to remain chaste (virginal). He feels she is wasting her beauty by not wanting to sleep with him. It is debatable whether Romeo is really in love or simply driven by his sexual desires.

In Act 1 scene 4, Romeo debates whether love is tender or rough. In his view it presents a **dichotomy** (opposing values). He sums up love's opposing qualities: it can be something gentle and 'tender', but it can also be dangerous and can hurt. The image of a thorn pricking sums this up clearly as a rose can be beautiful, but it has a dangerous side with its sharp thorns. The consequences of Romeo's love for Juliet can also be linked to the more violent pricking of Tybalt's sword as he kills Mercutio.

Love is described by Benvolio as 'gentle', but also 'tyrannous and rough in proof!' (1.1 160–61). Romeo feels that love and hate go closely together. They are both strong emotions and can cause just as many problems as each other:

> O brawling love, O loving hate!   (1.1 167)

Mercutio's attitude towards love is entirely negative. He sees it as unmanning

Romeo and turning him into an 'ape' or a fool (see *Characterisation* for a full discussion of this).

Although there is evidence in the play that Paris loves Juliet, particularly in his reaction to her death in Act 5 scene 3, Juliet clearly does not love Paris and, as a result, does not wish to marry him. She states, 'He shall not make me there a joyful bride' (3.5 117). Her attitude to marriage, however, is out of line with what is expected from her and this is best exemplified by her father's threats to throw her out of the family home if she refuses to marry Paris. Such extreme behaviour could be Shakespeare's comment on how wrong this form of arranged marriage is.

The love between Romeo and Juliet is a romantic form of love. Their feelings are deep and there is almost a spirituality about it. They give themselves so completely to each other that nothing else matters. Their love is passionate, but the Friar urges moderation from Romeo, whose over-passionate nature has urged him to marry Juliet speedily and regardless of the consequences. The Friar warns Romeo of the dangers of marrying too quickly in Act 2 scene 6.

The constant advice against passionate and intense love which both Romeo and Juliet are given throughout the play from family, friends and advisors, might be argued to be the key to why the play ends in tragedy. However, it is not just the young, but also the old that encourage this union, as both the Nurse and the Friar help the marriage on.

Fate, fortune, responsibility

Many of the play's events are seen by the majority of the characters as the result of fate or destiny.
- Romeo blames fortune and the stars.
- The Friar blames destiny and time.
- Montague and Capulet blame each other.
- Mercutio blames the Capulets and the Montagues.
- Tybalt blames Romeo.
- Paris blames Romeo.

Shakespeare creates and explores his characters' attitudes to the seemingly higher powers of fate and destiny, and to one another, inviting the audience to consider whether they might be rather too quick to shrug off personal responsibility.

It could be argued that it is destiny that Romeo and Juliet fall deeply in love on their first meeting. However, the nature of Romeo's love for Juliet is clearly questionable given his previous assertions to Benvolio about his undying devotion to Rosaline. Shakespeare has ensured that the audience

Grade *booster*

More effective answers will explore the varied images of love presented in the play. Capulet, for example, sees marriage as being a commodity, and does not seem to mind if a couple are not deeply in love. These views are perhaps reflected in his own marriage with Lady Capulet, which is dutiful, rather than a close and loving marriage. This equally reflects a business-like attitude to love and marriage which was common in English society in 1595.

Key *quotation*

These violent delights have violent ends

And in their triumph die like fire and powder,

Which as they kiss consume.

(2.6 9–11)

is aware of Juliet's extreme youth and her inexperience in matters of the heart. Furthermore, she has just told her mother that she has not thought about marrying but will do as her mother wishes in 'looking to like' Paris. It is notable here, though, that she makes no promises to her mother and is quite clever in her answer, adding that all important '*if* looking liking move'. This doubt, if it is one, seems completely cleared up the minute she sees Romeo. In her balcony soliloquy, Juliet speaks of Romeo's 'dear perfection', and declares that she will follow him through the world if only he would tell her he loves her. She has nothing other than 'looks' to go on, but that seems enough. She also seems to have forgotten her implied promise to her mother not to engage her affections further than her mother authorises: 'But no more deep will I endart mine eye/Than your consent gives strength to make it fly', although she is referring to Paris here.

Juliet is perfectly aware at this stage that her parents wish her to marry another man and she also knows who Romeo is — she states that she 'must' love a loathed enemy. Both make clear that they feel they have no choice but to love one another. But this does not mean that Shakespeare is agreeing with this. He seems to be inviting us to question precisely the degree to which people, including Romeo and Juliet, do have choices in life. The eternal question of whether or not we can choose who we love is definitely raised here. However, there is another issue Shakespeare may be inviting us to consider, and that is that even if we cannot choose who we love, surely we can choose what we do about it. Juliet tells Romeo in no uncertain terms that if his intentions are not 'honourable' and his 'purpose marriage', she would rather he left her 'to her grief'. This shows she is quite capable of choosing whether to take the love she feels further or not.

It might also be considered an unfortunate coincidence that the two young lovers happen to be members of the two feuding families, which will cause them great difficulty. But here again, the question is begged as to whose fault it is that the two families are feuding. Not Romeo's or Juliet's, for sure, but not fate, destiny or the stars either. The feud is caused by human and not superhuman forces. The older generation aren't exactly good role models in terms of accepting responsibility for their own actions: old Montague and Capulet with their petty feud, the Friar with his meddling and the Nurse with her childishly enthusiastic involvement in orchestrating Juliet's 'love' life.

It could be argued that 'fate' ensures that the Friar's letter is not delivered, but had it not been for the Friar's plan in the first place, there would have been no need of the letter. Again, it is human decisions and actions that set events in train, not superhuman intervention.

The Friar appears at the tomb moments after Romeo has killed himself and just as Juliet wakes up. He blames this 'mischance' on 'an unkind hour', but does not consider that had he not given Juliet the potion in the first place, this would not have happened. There is great **irony** in the Friar telling Romeo that if men cannot be constant in their loves, it is not surprising that 'women fall', meaning are unfaithful to their men. The irony lies in the fact that the Friar advises Romeo to act 'wisely and slow' and yet hastens their marriage through and makes decisions that most in the audience would see as anything but wise. He has also accused Romeo of being unmanly in his tears when he learns of his banishment, yet runs away the moment he fears being discovered and leaves Juliet alone in the tomb with the corpse of the man he knows she loves so much. Finally, the Friar as a member of the church is in a position of double trust: he is not only Romeo's adviser, but one who is meant to set the moral standards for his society. Yet he marries two young people without their parents' permission in the full knowledge that this would not be accepted by either family. With the adults in the play behaving in this way, the audience may well feel, what hope is there for the youngsters?

The Prologue pronounces Romeo and Juliet as 'a pair of star-cross'd lovers', but it is significant that the sonnet begins with man (the feud between the Montagues and the Capulets) not star-made strife. When taking an overview of the play, everything that happens to the young lovers can be attributed to human causes.

Arguably, fate's biggest role is when Romeo kills himself just before Juliet wakes up, paving the way for the complete tragedy at the end. Even here, though, one can't help but wonder whether Shakespeare did not intend us to see that had the impetuous Romeo sought out the Friar first to hear what had happened, the ending would have been different.

This is a tragedy and so Shakespeare will have intended us to see the outcome as anything but the result of a single cause, be it an outside force such as destiny, or an internal one such as a personal characteristic. What happens, as in any tragedy, is through a complex intertwining of many different factors — the end comes about inevitably. This inevitability need have nothing to do with destiny or any force outside of human nature.

It is interesting that at the end of the play, the Prince and old Montague and Capulet do finally take on board their own responsibility in having set the tragedy in motion, with the Prince for 'winking at' (turning a blind eye to) their 'discords' and Capulet and Montague for the feud that has caused them to lose their children. The fact that social harmony is restored only when personal responsibility is accepted and this is the note that the play ends upon is a powerful argument for its being one of Shakespeare's central themes in this play.

Grade *booster*

Higher grade answers may consider the structural role of the theme of fate. The audience always knows that Romeo and Juliet will die at the end of the play. Every time a character feels threatened by fate, the audience gets to feel more knowledgeable than them. In many ways, the audience is in the position of the higher power that so many of the characters fear in the play.

Pause for thought

How might the play's message of personal responsibility be relevant today?

Are adults always the best role models for young people?

Are priests or clergymen always going to give the best advice?

> **Key quotation**
>
> Put up your swords, you know not what you do.
>
> (1.1 56)

Friendship and enemies

Romeo, Mercutio and Benvolio are close friends, something which is evident from the start of the play. Shakespeare has created three characters who complement each other: Mercutio is aggressive and loves to argue, Benvolio is always looking for peace and Romeo has a rash desire to be in love. It seems that these differences do not matter when they are together, but their friendship group is under threat as Romeo has already deserted them for Rosaline and he does so again when he meets Juliet.

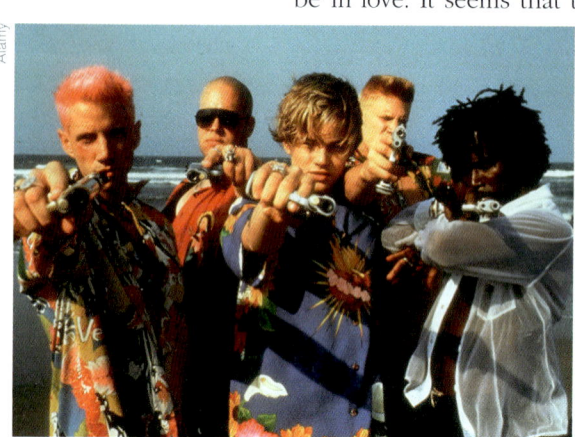

There is a hint that Mercutio is in love with Romeo (see *Characterisation* — Mercutio — for a detailed discussion of this). It has been suggested by several critics that Mercutio uses his Queen Mab fairy story to seduce Romeo, but Romeo does not understand and Mercutio has to give up, frustrated, admitting that he talks 'of dreams' (1.4 96).

Mercutio and Benvolio seem to need Romeo with them to have a good time and when just the two of them are together they discuss Romeo and do not seem to function properly as a group, both deciding to go to bed rather than to continue to search for Romeo in Act 2 scene 1.

> **Pause for thought**
>
> To what extent could the relationships between the Friar and Romeo, and Juliet and the Nurse be considered friendships?

While Romeo's friendship with his 'boys' is strong, the enemy rivalry with the Capulets has damaging strength. Throughout the play there is the threat of violence from Tybalt's continual attempts to cause chaos, whether it is at Capulet's party in Act 1 scene 5 or on the streets in Act 1 scene 1 and Act 3 scene 1. Benvolio tries to diffuse the tensions in both Act 1 scene 1 and Act 3 scene 1.

Romeo does not want any part in the feud and walks away from the violence in Act 3 scene 1. We know this is because of his marriage to Juliet, but he cannot tell anyone else this, which causes Mercutio to step in for Romeo's 'honour'. It is ironic that by trying to stop the fight, Romeo unwittingly causes the death of his close friend.

> **Key quotation**
>
> O brother Montague, give me thy hand...
>
> (5.3 296)

Families and conflict

Shakespeare opens both the Prologue and the first scene of the play with a focus on the feud. Against this backdrop of hate, a strong love forms, a juxtaposition of opposite emotions.

The power of a name, and what it represents, obsesses Tybalt who seems convinced that the Montagues are out to destroy the Capulets:

Themes

> Uncle, this is a Montague, our foe:
> A villain that is hither come in spite,
> To scorn at our solemnity this night. (1.5 60–62)

In Act 1 scene 5 Juliet asks herself, 'wherefore [why] art thou Romeo' because she knows that his name will cause problems. The strength of the feud means that only the deaths of the lovers, Montague's wife and Paris in the climactic final scene, convince Capulet and Montague that it must come to an end.

Shakespeare leaves his audience with some hope at the end of the play that Verona can now be a peaceful place. The feud, arguably, has caused the lovers to marry in secret, Tybalt and Mercutio's death, the brawl in Act 1 scene 1 and, we are told by the Prince, at least two other fights before the action of the play commences (1.1 80). The feud seems ever-present, either in the background or as the centre of the action, causing Romeo's banishment and the Friar's plans, which result in the deaths of Romeo and Juliet. The feud also gives Romeo and Juliet a valid reason for marrying secretly.

Family values are different in the world of the play from those we see today. This is most evident in Shakespeare's portrayal of the Capulet family, which is controlled by Capulet who often tells his wife and daughter what he expects of them. In asking his wife if she has delivered his 'decree' to Juliet regarding whom she will marry, Shakespeare's choice of word clearly underlines the degree to which he sees his wishes as law in his household. This repressive existence results in Juliet lying to them and disobeying her parents because she is in love with Romeo.

Grade *booster*

Higher grade answers might explore how Romeo is presented as part of a friendship group, rather than with his immediate family. This distances him from the feud and family issues in the play as he seems independent of his parents. By contrast, Juliet is in her family home for most of the play. How do these values differ today?

Review your learning

(Answers are given on p. 94.)

1. What are the main themes of the play?
2. What other themes might you suggest are dealt with in this play?
3. Which characters are used to explore the themes of love and marriage?
4. Which characters are used to explore the themes of fate, fortune and responsibility?
5. Which of these themes are still relevant today?

More interactive questions and answers online.

Tackling the assessments

- What sorts of questions will you have to answer?
- What is the best way to break down the question and plan your answer?
- How can you use PEE effectively?
- What are the differences between the higher and foundation tiers?
- How can you improve your grade?
- What do you have to do to get an A*?

Assessments

Depending on which exam board and specification you are following, you may have to respond to *Romeo and Juliet* in an English Literature examination or by Controlled Assessment. The sort of response you make in a Controlled Assessment may be written, spoken or multi-modal (a combination of written and spoken). Whichever board you are studying, the following table explains which unit the play appears in and gives you information about the sort of question you will face and whether you can take your text into the exam or Controlled Assessment. Remember, knowing the text well is important even if you can have the text with you.

AQA	Edexcel	WJEC	OCR	CCEA
Either Unit 3: The significance of Shakespeare and the English Literary Heritage — Controlled Assessment **Or** Unit 4: Approaching Shakespeare and the English Literary Heritage — Examination	Unit 3: Shakespeare and Contemporary Drama — Controlled Assessment	Unit 3: **Poetry and Drama (Literary Heritage)** — Controlled Assessment	Unit A661: Literary Heritage Linked Texts — Controlled Assessment	**Either** Unit 2: The Study of Drama and Poetry — Examination **Or** Unit 3: The Study of Linked Texts — Controlled Assessment

Tackling the assessments

AQA	Edexcel	WJEC	OCR	CCEA
Unit 3: Controlled Assessment task. A written response. The play must be compared to another text from the literary heritage. Some comment on a film/audio version is desirable. Unit 4: Exam. A written response. The play explored on its own.	A written response to a question out of a choice on characterisation, stagecraft, theme or relationships. Answers should compare the play text to a film/play or other version.	A written response to the play compared to poetry from the WJEC anthology. There must be some comment on a film/audio version linked in to the text.	A written response comparing the play text with a film, audio or live version of the play.	Unit 2: A written essay response to one question out of two. Unit 3: Controlled Assessment tasks will expect comparison between the play and a novel. Two tasks will be set, one based just on the Shakespeare play, the other comparing the two texts studied.
Un-annotated text allowed	Un-annotated text allowed Notes Dictionary/thesaurus Grammar and spell checker	Un-annotated text allowed	Un-annotated text allowed	Un-annotated texts allowed
Controlled Assessment = 3–4 hours 2,000 words Examination = 45 minutes	Approximately 2 hours	Up to 4 hours 2,000 words	Up to 3 hours 1,000 words	Controlled Assessment = up to 2 hours 30 minutes Examination = 1 hour
Controlled Assessment = 25% Literature mark Examination = 20% Literature mark	15% Literature mark	25% Literature mark	10% Literature mark	Controlled Assessment = 25% Literature mark Examination = 20% Literature mark

Marking

The marking of your responses varies according to the board and options your school or you have chosen. If you are studying *Romeo and Juliet* for examination, then an external examiner marks your response. If you are responding to it in a Controlled Assessment, your teacher marks your work and it is then moderated by someone else. In all cases, your ability to respond to the play in a critical way is important. Assessment Objectives for individual assessments are explained in the next section of the guide (see p. 76).

Essay writing: hints and tips

Whether you are responding in an exam or Controlled Assessment, knowing how to plan, structure and write an essay is vital. A typical essay contains:
- an introduction, where you suggest your line of argument
- the main body of the essay, where you develop it
- a conclusion, where you sum up your argument, saving a really good point until the end

A typical essay on a play should contain comments on many aspects of the work. You have to decide what is required on the basis of the individual question, but you should be prepared to write about:
- plot (related to the question)
- characterisation
- setting
- dialogue
- language
- purpose
- effectiveness
- mood
- point of view
- context
- staging

You need to offer textual support for any comments you make.

Pause for thought

A useful exercise is:
1. Write down in a notebook the key events of the play.
2. Write a one-paragraph description of each of the major characters.
3. Write a brief summary of what the writer set out to do.

Planning your answer

To help you with your planning it is important to have prepared yourself thoroughly for the examination.

Knowing your way around the text

No matter how good you are at writing essays, there is no substitute for knowing the text well. For AQA Unit 4 and CCEA Unit 2 you can take the book into the exam with you. If you are studying *Romeo and Juliet* as a text for Controlled Assessment, you can use a copy of the text when writing your answer, but it must not contain your notes. This means you could end up spending a long time trying to find an incident or a particular quotation unless you know where to find it beforehand.

The time you have for writing is short, so although you will gain no marks for re-telling the story, you should have a sound grasp of the following:

Tackling the assessments

- the main events
- the sequence in which they occur
- the part played by each character in them

Although you are not expected to label the acts and scenes of every reference/quotation you include, you do need to be able to make clear that you know who is saying what, to whom, when and why. In other words, do not quote out of context as it will reveal little understanding of anything.

The question

Breaking down the question

If you feel under pressure when writing your answer, it is tempting to read the question quickly and start writing a response immediately. Instead, you should read the question carefully, at least twice, and attempt to break it down into parts to work out exactly what you are being asked to do. This helps to ensure that you answer the question that is being asked. A useful technique is to underline the key words. You should practise underlining or highlighting the key words in every new question you meet.

Here is a higher-tier question (with key words underlined). It is an example of the sort of question that may appear on the AQA examination:

> **a** <u>How</u> does the <u>extract</u> from Act 1 scene 5 <u>highlight</u> some of the <u>themes</u> of the play?
> **b** Explain <u>how Shakespeare uses another scene</u> of the play to <u>develop</u> his <u>themes</u>.

You could break this down in the following way:
1. What are the themes reflected in this extract?
2. How does the scene contribute to these themes?
3. How does the relationship begin? The importance of looks?
4. How does Shakespeare use language and imagery to show Romeo and Juliet's feelings for each other?
5. What second scene can you choose which builds on the themes and ideas you have spotted here?

Sometimes the question is open to more than one interpretation. For the question above you can pick a number of different themes that are relevant here, including the nature of love, the importance of names, and the degree to which choices are possible, then and now.

You won't have time to deal with all of these options at great length in your essay, so you need to identify three or four main points you can write about well, and make these clear in your opening paragraph.

Grade *booster*

If the meaning of a question is still unclear to you, choose another question — if there is a choice. If you do tackle a question that you are unsure about, the important thing is to make your interpretation of it clear at the start of your essay.

ROMEO AND JULIET

The form of your plan

You may find it helpful to use a diagram of some sort — perhaps a **spider diagram** or **flow chart** (see the examples at **www.philipallan.co.uk/literatureguidesonline**). This may help you to keep your mind open to new ideas as you plan, so that you can slot them in. You could make a list instead. The important thing is to choose a method that works for you.

You will probably need to note important points down on paper before you arrange them. If you have made a spider diagram, arranging them is a simple matter of numbering the branches in the best possible order.

Referring to the author and title

You can refer to Shakespeare either by name (make sure you spell it correctly) or as 'the playwright'. You should never use his first name (William) — this sounds as if you know him personally. You can also save time by giving the play title in full the first time you refer to it, with 'R and J' in brackets after it, and then using the shorter title after that.

Grade *booster*

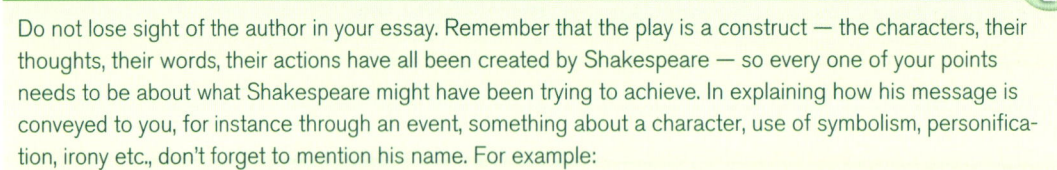

Do not lose sight of the author in your essay. Remember that the play is a construct — the characters, their thoughts, their words, their actions have all been created by Shakespeare — so every one of your points needs to be about what Shakespeare might have been trying to achieve. In explaining how his message is conveyed to you, for instance through an event, something about a character, use of symbolism, personification, irony etc., don't forget to mention his name. For example:

- Shakespeare makes it clear that xxx
- It is evident from xxx that Shakespeare is inviting the audience to consider xxx
- Here, the audience may well feel that Shakespeare is suggesting xxx

Writing in an appropriate style

Remember that you are expected to write in an *appropriate* way for a formal exam essay. Examiners' reports every year give a range of inappropriate language used by candidates. These instances can make amusing reading, but they lose marks. To use a technical term, you must write in a suitable **register**. This means:

- *not* using colloquial language or slang (except when quoting dialogue), e.g. 'Tybalt's a nasty piece of work. A bit of a toe-rag really.'
- *not* becoming too personal, e.g. 'Romeo is like my mate, right, 'cos he…'
- using suitable phrases for an academic essay, e.g. 'It could be argued that', not 'I reckon that…'

Tackling the assessments

The first person ('I')

It is perfectly appropriate to say 'I feel' or 'I think'. You *are* being asked for your opinion. Just remember that you are being asked for your opinion about *what* Shakespeare may have been trying to convey in his play (his themes) and *how* he does this (characters, events, language of the play). You are not being asked for your personal opinion about love, as such, but about what you think Shakespeare is saying about it and how.

Although your spelling, punctuation and grammar are not specifically targeted for assessment in English Literature, you cannot afford to forget that you will demonstrate your grasp of the play through the way you write, so take great care with this and don't be sloppy. If the examiner cannot understand what you are trying to say, they will not be able to give you credit for it.

Above all, remember that *essay writing is a skill and requires practice.*

> **Grade booster**
>
> Preface your opinion with phrases such as:
> - in my opinion
> - equally, another view might be
> - some may feel
> - it has been argued that
> - some critics suggest that
> - on the other hand
> - alternatively, one might say
> - however, it is notable that

Using PEE effectively

You need to make your initial **P**oint and back this up with **E**vidence from the play before **E**xplaining your idea further.

For example, the following is part of a good answer and with further development should gain a high mark:

> Write about how Shakespeare presents the theme of love in *Romeo and Juliet* and one other text. (possible AQA Controlled Assessment task)

Above all, Shakespeare presents love as a force so powerful that some are willing to die for it.**1** In the second love scene between Romeo and Juliet, where dawn is breaking and Juliet attempts to persuade Romeo that it is not the lark they are hearing, but 'the nightingale',**2** in order to persuade him to stay, he cries, 'Let me be ta'en, let me be put to death./I am content, so thou wilt have it so.'**3** Juliet too would rather '…go into a new-made grave/ And hide …with a dead man in his tomb' than marry Paris, in order to 'live an unstained wife'**3** to Romeo. She even cries 'I long to die'**3** before he comes up with his 'remedy'**3** to her situation. Both view their love as more important than life and are willing to sacrifice theirs in order to be prove their love for and keep faith with one another.**4**

However,**5** we also see that Shakespeare raises some questions about the exact nature of the love that Romeo and Juliet have for one another.**6** In particular, the structure of the play**7** is important in introducing Romeo at the start as suffering from unrequited love…**8**

1 Point made about the importance of love in the play

2 Contextualising the reference

3 Quotations — embedded as a part of the candidate's sentences

4 Unpacking or explaining the effect of the quotations — that is, what these words have made you think

5 Link word moving essay on

6 Next point

7 Bringing up a technique used to illustrate the theme

8 Lead up to next quotation

> **Grade *booster***
>
> It is important to make the individual quotations you select brief and to try to *embed* them as the candidate has done in this example. This will save you time, enabling you to bring up more points and so raise your grade.

Foundation and higher tiers

You will be entered for the exam at either the foundation or the higher tier. This does not apply to Controlled Assessment tasks.

Foundation tier

The foundation-tier questions are easier than those for the higher tier, but the highest grade you can get is a C. The skills you need for either tier are the same. Be especially careful not to do any of the things listed in 'What you will not gain marks for' on p. 79.

The foundation-tier examination questions may be based on characterisation rather than themes or style. They generally involve a number of bullet-point hints to offer a framework for your essay.

AQA-style question — exam/Controlled Assessment

Whether you are sitting the exam or answering a question as a Controlled Assessment task, the types of questions you are likely to be asked will be similar. The only difference is when and where you do the task.

> How does Shakespeare present and develop the relationship between Juliet and the Nurse?
> In your answer you may wish to consider:
> - what Juliet says to the Nurse
> - how the Nurse speaks about and to Juliet
> - the ways the Nurse helps Juliet

Plan

Use the bullet points to help you frame your answer. Think about:
- what scenes the two characters appear in
- what significant events happen involving them
- how they appear to feel about each other
- how the Nurse behaves with regard to Juliet
- how Juliet speaks and reacts to the Nurse
- the techniques and devices Shakespeare uses to reveal aspects of their relationship

Tackling the assessments

OCR-style question — Controlled Assessment

For the OCR specification you will be required to study the play and one film or audio version of it.

> Look again at Act 1 scene 1 and Act 3 scene 1 and watch the scenes from one or two film versions or listen to one or two audio versions.
>
> With close reference to the text, explore how conflict is presented in the film versions you have watched or the audio versions you have studied.
>
> Consider:
> - the thoughts and feelings of the characters
> - the way characters react to each other
> - the dramatic effect of the scenes

Plan

Include:
- how the characters interact with each other
- how the film captures or changes the mood or ideas intended in the original text (techniques used)
- how well or poorly you feel this represents Shakespeare's intentions in the original text
- a close exploration of language used by Shakespeare

WJEC-style question — Controlled Assessment

> Look at how Shakespeare presents Romeo and Juliet's first meeting.
> - Think about how they speak to each other.
> - Look at the poem X and how the writer presents the relationship between two people here.
> - What is your personal response to these two pieces of literature? Make links between the two texts.

Plan

You will need to compare the play with a poem, so ensure that you plan for this.

Focus on Act 1 scene 5 and:
- what Romeo and Juliet say to each other
- how they speak to each other
- explore some of the imagery used
- explore some of the other language devices Shakespeare uses
- remember to make your own personal response to the texts — this will give you a chance to comment on aspects of Romeo and Juliet's relationship throughout the rest of the play and on some of the themes presented in this section of the text

Edexcel-style question — Controlled Assessment

Explore the ways the theme of order versus chaos is presented in the Luhrmann film and the original text of *Romeo and Juliet*.

Use examples from the texts in your response.

Think about:
- how order or chaos is presented
- what scenes reveal this theme most clearly
- what literary devices Shakespeare uses to develop this theme
- how the director chooses to present the theme

Plan

First, you will need to think about which parts of the play are best to examine when looking at order and chaos — Act 1 scene 1 and Act 3 scene 1 are good choices, showing both elements. Try not to deal with too many scenes as you will not be able to look at ideas in detail.

Once you have chosen your scenes:
- explore how order/disorder is shown in the film version and the text
- compare both the action and the language used
- examine and explore how the order is re-established by the Prince in both scenes — look at what he says and how he says it
- explore how the director chooses to show these scenes

CCEA-style question — exam

This question is about **the Friar.**

How does Shakespeare **present** the Friar? Explore how far you agree that he is helpful to Romeo and Juliet?

What do you think of him? Give reasons for your answer.

In your answer, include some comments on:
- how he is viewed by other characters
- his plans for Romeo and Juliet
- his good qualities
- his bad qualities

You should discuss Shakespeare's use of language and dramatic techniques.

Plan

As this question has several parts you need to make sure you include relevant comments on each section.

Look at how Shakespeare presents the Friar, thinking about language, the way he speaks and what others say about him.

Tackling the assessments

Explore what he does for Romeo and Juliet. How helpful is he? You might consider the failure of his plans — is this his fault? Why does he help them so much? Should he have helped as much as he does?

When you discuss your opinion of the Friar try to explore his good qualities and contrast this with his negative side.

Higher tier

At higher tier you may not be given bullet-point hints to help you. If you are, think about them and consider using them as the basis of your essay plan. If you are not given any bullet-point hints, you should write them yourself in your essay plan, so you need to think carefully about what the question is asking you to do. There may be several elements to the question (see 'Breaking down the question' above).

For boards using Controlled Assessment only, the tasks can be the same for both higher- and foundation-tier students, although foundation-tier students may be given more guidance.

Below are some examples of higher-tier questions.

> **Pause for thought**
>
> Consider the following aspects of the Friar's character:
> - He is helpful.
> - He is holy.
> - He wants the feud to end.
> - He tries to escape at the end.
> - He hides away.
> - He deals with poisons and potions.

AQA-style question — exam

> How are the relationships between the two families presented in *Romeo and Juliet*?

AQA-style question — Controlled Assessment

> Explore how two texts present people who are in love with each other.
> - Explore the ways texts develop ideas about people in love.
> - Compare the ways in which Shakespeare, in *Romeo and Juliet*, and one other author you have studied explore the problems love can cause.

Plan

Your precise plan will depend on the second text you have studied, but you will need to find links between the two.
- Who are the lovers?
- What are the problems with love in each text?
- How is this presented in the two texts?
- What similarities and differences are there?

CCEA — exam

> This question is about **the Friar**.
>
> How does Shakespeare **present** the Friar? Explore how far you agree that he is helpful to Romeo and Juliet? What do you think of him? Give reasons for your answer.
>
> You should discuss Shakespeare's use of language and dramatic techniques.

ROMEO AND JULIET

Plan

You will need to devise your own bullet points to help you structure your answer and include all the relevant areas to secure the highest mark.

You are analysing *how* the Friar is presented, so you will need to consider all of Shakespeare's devices that give us our impression of the Friar: the ordering of events in the play (structure), what the Friar says and does (characterisation/language), what other characters say and how they react to him (characterisation/language).

Improving your grade

Most students can immediately make some improvement in grade by recognising what it is that they are being asked to do. All written tasks can be broken down into these simple areas:
- What did the writer set out to do?
- How did the writer go about doing it?
- Was the writer successful?

Many students fall into retelling the story. You need to refer to the story to make your points, but if all you do in your essay is retell it, you aren't actually giving any opinion on what you think Shakespeare has written it for. You must show the examiner that you understand the meanings he wished to convey through the play. The play is simply a means through which Shakespeare conveys the subtext — his thoughts and ideas about the world he lived in — to his audience, inviting them to reflect on aspects of it themselves.

When you come to discuss the ways Shakespeare went about achieving his aims, you need to select parts of the play that enable you to talk about a number of different ways in which he puts his ideas across to you. You might highlight a use of language that reveals something about Shakespeare's treatment of personal responsibility versus destiny. You might comment on a particular character's action that expresses Shakespeare's idea that overbearing authority can be harmful, leading to deceit and lies. The structuring of the play could make a point, for instance the early stress laid on Romeo's infatuation with Rosaline might be argued as Shakespeare's means of highlighting the physical, and hence shallow, nature of attraction for this character, putting an interesting twist on the way we respond to Romeo's 'love' for Juliet so quickly thereafter.

Grade-C candidates:
- understand and demonstrate how writers use ideas, themes and settings in texts to affect the reader
- respond personally to the effects of language, structure and form

Tackling the assessments

- refer to textual details to support their views and reactions
- explain the relevance and impact of connections and comparisons between texts
- show awareness of some of the social, cultural and historical contexts of texts and of how this influences their meanings for contemporary and modern readers
- convey ideas clearly and appropriately

Grade-A* candidates:

- respond enthusiastically and critically to texts, showing imagination and originality in developing alternative approaches and interpretations
- confidently explore and evaluate how language, structure and form contribute to writers' varied ways of presenting ideas, themes and settings and how they achieve specific effects on readers
- make illuminating connections and comparisons between texts
- identify and comment on the impact of the social, cultural and historical contexts of texts on different readers and times
- convey ideas persuasively and cogently, supporting them with apt textual reference

Getting an A*

To reach the highest level you need to consider whether the writer has been successful. If, for example, you think Shakespeare set out to explore the ways people react to difficult situations and invites his audience to consider this question, do you think he achieved this purpose? Has he made you think about this? How and where?

You need to make your points clearly and succinctly and convince the examiner that your viewpoint is really your own, and a valid one, with constant and careful reference to the text. This will be aided by the use of short and apposite (meaning really relevant) quotations, skilfully embedded in your answer along the way (see *Sample essays*).

Review your learning

(Answers are given on p. 94.)
1. What is an essay?
2. Why is it important to plan your answer?
3. How do you use PEE effectively?
4. What qualities do you need in an essay to achieve an A*?

More interactive questions and answers online.

Assessment Objectives and skills

All GCSE examinations are pinned to specific areas of learning that the examiners want to be sure the candidates have mastered. These are known as Assessment Objectives or AOs. If you are studying *Romeo and Juliet* as an examination text for either AQA or CCEA, the examiner marking your exam essay will be trying to give you marks, but will only be able to do so if you succeed in fulfilling the key AOs for English Literature.

Assessment Objectives

The Assessment Objectives that you are assessed on are:
- **AO1:** (Candidates must) respond to texts critically and imaginatively; select and evaluate relevant textual detail to illustrate and support interpretations.
- **AO2:** (Candidates must) explain how language, structure and form contribute to writers' presentation of ideas, themes and settings.
- **AO3:** (Candidates must) make comparisons and explain links between texts, evaluating writers' different ways of expressing meaning and achieving effects.
- **AO4:** (Candidates must) relate texts to their social, cultural and historical contexts; explain how texts have been influential and significant to self and other readers in different contexts and at different times.

The examining boards share out their attention to AOs in slightly different ways.

Examination:
- AQA assesses AO1 and AO2.
- CCEA assesses AO1 and AO2.

Controlled Assessment:
- AQA assesses AO1, AO2, AO3 and AO4.
- WJEC assesses AO1, AO2 and AO3.
- OCR assesses AO1 and AO3.

Assessment Objectives and skills

- Edexcel assesses AO1, AO2 and AO3.
- CCEA assesses AO1, AO3 and AO4.

Whatever the board, you are likely to impress the examiner if you show some awareness of the 'social, cultural and historical contexts' that have influenced the play.

What skills do you need to show?

Let's break the Assessment Objectives down to see what they mean.

AO1

(Candidates must) respond to texts critically and imaginatively; select and evaluate relevant textual detail to illustrate and support interpretations.

- **'respond to texts critically'**: this means you must say what you think of the text and why. You should realise that the writer has made choices and give your views on how effective these choices are.
- **'imaginatively'**: this means your points need to be interesting and exploratory of the text and its potential meanings, taking into account that there may be more than one interpretation of an idea or moment.
- **'select…relevant textual detail to illustrate and support interpretations'**: this means giving short quotations from the text, or referring to details in the text, to support your views.
- **'evaluate'**: means commenting on how well you think the textual detail you have selected has achieved what you have said you think Shakespeare's purpose is.

AO2

(Candidates must) explain how language, structure and form contribute to writers' presentation of ideas, themes and settings.

- **'Explain how language, structure and form…'**:
  - The word '**language**' refers to Shakespeare's use of words. For example, when Romeo first sees Juliet in Act 1 scene 5, Shakespeare uses a lot of imagery to convey his response to Juliet's beauty. When Romeo says she is 'Like a rich jewel in an Ethiope's ear', Shakespeare uses a simile to emphasise her value and rare beauty.
  - The word '**structure**' refers to how the play is put together, the order of events and the introduction of characters, as well as the length of various sections and scenes, including what is juxtaposed with what (see *Plot and structure*). For example, the Chorus's speech at the start of Act 2 has structural importance. It occurs just after Romeo and Juliet have met and fallen in love, but before the

balcony scene. This interjection at this point reinforces the fact that Romeo has been 'bewitched by the charm of looks', an important emphasis revealing what Shakespeare seems to be suggesting about the nature of young love, or Romeo's love at least.
- The word '**form**' asks you to comment on *Romeo and Juliet* as a play. Its dramatic form allows the writer to create a text that will have a visual impact, making it appealing to an audience by exciting and involving them in the action and playing on their emotions. Imagine the impact of being only yards away from the death scene at the end of the play, or the fight scenes; a film creates a necessary distance, but with a play, the audience shares the same air space as the actors and so the atmosphere will be charged with the emotions displayed on stage. Consider each scene in the light of this, and you will understand why many writers opt for a play as their medium of communication of their ideas.
- **'…contribute to writers' presentation of ideas, themes and settings'**: the word '**ideas**' refers to what Shakespeare is writing about and trying to say in the play. It is through his uses of his form, its structure, setting and its language that Shakespeare reveals his themes to us, so it is essential that you realise that these two aspects go hand in hand. (See *Themes* and *Characterisation* for detailed discussion of these aspects; see *Context* for discussion of setting.)

AO3

(Candidates must) make comparisons and explain links between texts, evaluating writers' different ways of expressing meaning and achieving effects.
- **'make comparisons'**: the most important aspect of this Assessment Objective is how you compare the texts you are writing about. A text doesn't just mean the written play, but can be a film, audio or play version if you are comparing the text with another version of the play. You will need to compare the play to some poetry if you are studying the WJEC specification and the play needs to be compared to any other text you have studied if you are doing the AQA Controlled Assessment tasks. If you are doing the CCEA Controlled Assessment you will need to compare the play to a prose text. For the OCR and Edexcel Controlled Assessment tasks you must compare the play text to a film/theatre or audio version of the play.
- **'explain links between texts'**: this means you need to draw the examiner's attention to similarities or differences between the texts you are analysing.

Assessment Objectives and skills

- You will need to find how the writers/directors have '**different ways of expressing meaning**' by looking at language, directorial devices, acting performances and a range of other presentational devices, both on the written page and otherwise.

AO4

(Candidates must) relate texts to their social, cultural and historical contexts; explain how texts have been influential and significant to self and other readers in different contexts and at different times.

- **'relate texts to their social, cultural and historical contexts'**: this means you must show you understand how knowledge of what was going on at the time the play was written shapes your interpretation of events, characters and the language of the play. For example, knowing how love and marriage were viewed at this time is vital if we are to understand Shakespeare's intentions in his presentation of Juliet's situation in the play.
- **'explain how texts have been influential and significant to self and other readers in different contexts and at different times'**: this is checking whether you are aware, for instance, that an audience in the 1590s will have seen the play differently from an audience today as people have different values now and will react differently to the ideas expressed within the play.
- The word '**influential**' means how a text or idea within a text can affect a reader's thoughts and ideas about something, both when the play was written and now. For example, you might suggest that the idea of personal responsibility explored in the text is still significant today, as many still believe in fate, God's will, or the stars dictating our lives and therefore do not take responsibility for what they do or what happens as a result of their actions. However, you might also say that as attitudes towards marriage have changed so radically, a modern audience's response to Juliet's father may be different to that of the Elizabethan audience.

> **Grade booster**
>
> Finding connections and comparisons throughout your essay will help you achieve the highest marks.

Remember, do not treat your English Literature writing as though you were producing a history essay. Your task is to write about the play.

What you will not gain marks for

- **Retelling the story.** You can be sure that the examiner marking your essay knows the story inside out. A key feature of the lowest grades is 'retelling the story'. Don't do it.
- **Quoting long passages.** Remember, the point is that every reference and piece of quotation must serve a very specific point you are

making. If you quote at length, the examiner will have to guess which bit of the quotation you mean to serve your point. Don't impose work on the examiner — be explicit about exactly which words you have found specific meaning in. Keep quotes short and smart.

- **Merely identifying literary devices.** You will never gain marks simply for identifying literary devices such as a simile or a use of rhyme. You will only gain marks by identifying these features *and* saying why the author has used them and how effective you think they are.
- **Giving unsubstantiated opinions.** The examiner will be keen to give you marks for your opinions, but only if they are supported by reasoned argument and references to the text. Hence you will get no marks for writing: 'Everyone thinks that Romeo falls in love with Juliet far too easily.' But you will get marks for: 'Romeo has just been feeling sad because of his failed relationship with Rosaline so the fact that he suddenly forgets about her and is totally infatuated with Juliet makes him seem fickle and rather too free with his emotions.'

Purpose and audience

One key element of any good answer is comment on purpose and audience. This means:

- Why did the writer write *this*?
- What is the motivation behind the piece?
- Who were the intended audience?
- Has the writer been successful?

Remember to discuss these points in each literature essay that you write and you will find yourself moving up the grades.

Review your learning

(Answers are given on p. 94.)
1. What is AO1 assessing?
2. What is AO2 assessing?
3. What is AO3 assessing?
4. What is AO4 assessing?
5. Which board are you doing and what AOs should you be focusing on?
6. What should you not do in your answers?

More interactive questions and answers online.

Sample essays

Structuring your essay

Think in terms of your essay having three sections:
1. beginning (introduction)
2. middle (development)
3. end (conclusion)

You need good ideas to write a good essay, but you also need to demonstrate that you can put them together in a logical order, developing them to reach your conclusion. Here are some hints for each section of the essay.

Beginning (introduction)

Limit yourself to an opening paragraph of no more than about 100 words. This should do one thing: answer the question in essence, otherwise known as setting out your thesis. The development of why this thesis is correct comes in the body of the essay and its conclusion.

Beware of starting your essay in a way that forces you to write a list. Consider this generic WJEC question:

> Many plays explore the relationship between men and women. Select a relationship between a man and a woman in the play you have studied and compare it with the way a poet presents a similar relationship.

You should not begin by writing 'The way that the relationship between men and women is explored is…'. If you do this your whole essay will have to be a simple list. It is far better to write: 'The relationship between men and women is explored in several ways. One of these is…'. This structure allows you to develop the essay logically while still keeping the question closely in focus.

Middle (development)

If you have made a good plan, you know what you are doing and can follow your plan, point by point, presenting your argument with appropriate evidence to back it up.

Part of the secret to good organisation is to plan properly in the first place, arranging your points in a logical way so that one leads on from the next. However, it is also important to use appropriate link words and phrases. These **signpost** your ideas, giving the reader an idea of what is coming next and how it relates to the previous idea. Look at the words

> **Grade booster**
>
> *Do not* begin your essay with phrases such as 'In this essay I am going to…'. Try to reflect the question but do not simply turn it around.

and phrases in the table below. Try not to begin any two paragraphs in a row with the same phrase, and certainly not two sentences in a row.

> **Pause for thought**
>
> It is important not to overuse any of the phrases in the table. Can you think of any other words or phrases you could use?

Word/phrase	Idea it contains
However	An exception is coming
Yet	*Yet* can be used without the comma
Despite this	
Nevertheless	
Nonetheless	Signals the development of a point
On the other hand	Signals a balanced alternative, e.g. '*On the other hand*, it could be argued that…'. Useful for showing you realise that different interpretations of the text are valid
By contrast	Signals a difference
Similarly	Signals something that is the same
Another example	Signals further illustration of your point
In addition	Signals a reinforcement of your point
Above all	Introduces the most important point you want to make

End (conclusion)

The conclusion should draw your arguments to a logical close, but should not simply repeat what you have already said. The conclusion should, above all, refer back to the question, showing that you have not lost sight of it. Make sure you save a really good point that you feel will clinch, or really underline the central point you have been trying to argue throughout, for your conclusion.

Question 1 (AQA Controlled Assessment)
Topic: themes and ideas

Explore the ways Shakespeare in *Romeo and Juliet*, and one other author you have studied, present conflict.

A* answer

The most apparent way in which Shakespeare presents conflict in 'Romeo and Juliet' is through the creation of two families, the Montagues and the Capulets,

Sample essays

whose long-standing feud has an impact not only on themselves, but on all of Verona.**1** We are never told what their conflict is about, just that this violence in the streets of Verona has been 'bred', or caused, by 'an airy word';**2** a mere nothing.**3** How Shakespeare presents us with this piece of information in the original text is revealing.**4** First, it is delivered to us through Prince Escalus,**5** a character high in status and whose name signifies the scales of justice;**6** the audience is therefore encouraged by Shakespeare to put store in what he says.**7** Secondly, his apportioning of blame is equal. He states that not one, but 'three civil brawls'**8** have been caused:

'By thee, old Capulet, and Montague,'**9**

These words are set out on the same line to stress their equal blameworthiness**10** and the commas operate as important pauses or caesura,**11** to allow the audience to take in**12** that it is not simply one of them that has caused the ongoing feud, but the pair of them. By doing this, Shakespeare stresses that the seed of this conflict lies with the heads of these households who, arguably, ought to know better.**13** This point is reinforced by Shakespeare in the way he ends the play**14** with their final acceptance of shared responsibility, symbolised**15** by their each volunteering to erect a monument to the memory of the other's child,**16** the 'poor sacrifices of (their) enmity'.**17** The word 'sacrifice' underlines how their children died untimely and violent deaths, metaphorically speaking, at their hands.**18**

1 Question addressed clearly — first 'way' offered for discussion

2 First use of quotation, skilfully embedded, short and serving to illustrate the point

3 What the words tell us, i.e. their effect on the audience

4 Reference to AO2 (language, structure and form)

5 Specific about method Shakespeare uses

6 Explanation of how he uses the character

7 Effect of these uses of character

8 Quotation on the way to further illustrate point

9 Quotation to be analysed for use of language point (AO2)

10 First suggestion of how it works

11 Second analytical point related to this use of language

12 Effect of this

13 Extending analysis of effect on audience — reference to Shakespeare's possible intention

14 Reinforcement of the point with further reference to text

15 A further literary technique

16 Explanation of how symbolism works here

17 More brief quotation to validate point

18 Explanation of the effect of this choice of word

In the middle (development) section of the essay, the candidate continued with a link to their other text.

By contrast,**19** in 'The Other Woman' by Liz Lochhead, we see that the conflict is an internal one**20** where 'the other woman'**21** that is seen as competition by the narrative voice in the poem, actually 'lies'**22**, within her. Here language is used skilfully with the word 'lies' being placed alone on a line for emphasis, similar to the way Shakespeare used the line placement of words to stress his meaning.**23** Here, though, the word also carries a double entendre, in that this other woman does not just 'lie' metaphorically speaking between she and her partner, but is also the cause of lies, as in untruths, between her and her partner**24** that lead to conflict.

Shakespeare also**25** makes use of double entendres or puns to show how conflict may …

19 Link phrase

20 Focus on key word in question — signposting for the examiner that the response is still on target

21 Quotation

22 Quotation

23 Comparison of technique

24 Difference of technique

25 Link phrase

Look at the link phrases the candidate uses. This is good technique. The examiner should never start to read a paragraph and think 'Hang on — how did we get here?' The candidate then followed their plan, making a series of points before reaching a solid conclusion.

26 Comparison flagged up

27 Awareness of form

28 Awareness of perspective

29 Awareness of central feature of these forms

30 Further development — original thinking

31 Candidate's opinion about what the authors are saying about conflict

32 Further development — original thinking

Shakespeare and Lochhead explore conflict from different angles and perspectives**26**; one uses a poem, the other a play**27** and of course one is modern female and the other an Elizabethan male!**28** However, Lochhead, principally through her choices of words and where she places them and Shakespeare, principally through his characters,**29** seem to agree on one thing; the roots of all conflict lie not in any grand plan being orchestrated by outside influences, but in human nature itself.**30** To conclude, I would guess that both of these writers would agree that human beings are the architects of their own conflicts;**31** which doesn't of course mean that either think there is much we can do to prevent this!**32**

Question 2 (CCEA)

How does Shakespeare present the Nurse?
Think about:
- her role in the play
- how she helps the Capulet family
- what you think about her

Remember to write about Shakespeare's use of language and form.

C grade conclusion

The Nurse, overall, is loyal to Juliet and tries to do everything she can to help her out, even if it gets her in trouble. Shakespeare shows her loyalty to Juliet throughout the play.

This is a C-grade standard conclusion and would need to sum up the role of the Nurse in terms of Shakespeare's intentions for her character and the whole play in much more detail to gain a higher grade. As it stands, it would be easy to argue against this assessment of the Nurse's character as it is a little too simplistic and generalised.

Using quotations and referring to the text

One of the most important elements of writing an English Literature essay is your use of quotations to support your comments. You will have the text in front of you in the examination, so knowing the words themselves is not an issue. The key to success is to be selective.

Sample essays

There are five basic principles to remember regarding your use of quotations:
1 Keep them brief.
2 Use them often.
3 Place inverted commas around them.
4 Save time by embedding them.
5 If longer, set them out as you see them on the printed page.

Quotations should be used to illustrate and develop the line of thought in your essay. Your comments should not duplicate what is in your quotation. For example do not write:
Juliet's reply to Paris is ironic, as she already is a wife to Romeo. She hides the truth to protect herself from further problems:

'That may be, sir, when I may be a wife.' (4.1 19)

It would be far more effective to write:
'Juliet's response to Paris: 'That may be, sir, when I may be a wife.' (4.1 19) is ironic in its ambiguity; the audience knows she already is a wife, but Paris will of course take this as maidenly modesty.

The most sophisticated way of using the writer's words is to embed them into your sentence:
Juliet's comment to Paris about his calling her his 'wife' only when she 'may be a wife', is rich in irony as what Paris will interpret as shyness or modesty is really her way of saying that she 'may' never be his 'wife' as she already is one to another man.

When you use quotations in this way, you save time and show the examiner that you are aware of specifically which piece of language illustrates your point.

This does not mean that you should never use longer sections of quotation. Sometimes your points may require it. If you do need to do this, remember that you should set out the quotation just as it appears on the page. For example, Juliet's lines below:

> Good pilgrim, you do wrong your hand too much,
> Which mannerly devotion shows in this;
> For saints have hands that pilgrims' hands do touch,
> And palm to palm is holy palmers' kiss. (1.5 96–99)

Referring to the text

Remember also that it is not always necessary to use a quotation. If you cannot recall accurately the quotation you want or cannot find it, it is often just as good to refer to it. For example:

> **Grade booster**
>
> Practise choosing quotations to support your views about what Shakespeare is saying. Keep a quotations book in which you write down useful words and phrases to strengthen your knowledge of the text.

> **Grade booster**
>
> Look again at the A* answer on conflict and pay particular attention to the way the candidate has used quotation.

When, just before the Capulets' party, Romeo tells Mercutio about his fears of some terrible consequence should he go, Shakespeare is highlighting the superstition so common to his age.

Here, the reference is explored in a way that shows the language of the text has been understood.

Some further sections of sample essays are given below. In each case, examiner's comments are provided. Look at the grade-C responses first. You should then set about improving these sections yourself. Once you have done this, look at the A*-grade responses and compare the kinds of approach in these with the ones that you used.

There is no single correct way to approach an answer, but the higher-level responses should give you ideas about how to construct your own.

Question 3 (WJEC)

Topic: character

Look at how Shakespeare presents Romeo and Juliet's first meeting in *Romeo and Juliet*. Think about how they speak to each other.
Look at the poem X and how the writer presents the relationship between two people here.
What is your personal response to the two pieces of literature? Make links between the two texts.

Grade-C essay
Romeo and Juliet fall in love the moment they meet in Act 1 scene 5.

This opening reflects the demands of the question and makes it clear that the candidate is going to focus on the first meeting of Romeo and Juliet. It also avoids falling into the trap of writing a list. (Weaker candidates would probably put the word 'because' after the words 'the moment they meet in Act 1 scene 5' and end up writing a list.)

The logical thing to do next is to tackle how Shakespeare presents their first meeting, to look at how the characters speak to each other and to make sure you bring in the poetry you need to cover (WJEC candidates only), making suitable comparisons as you progress.

1 Accurate point about character and a general point on the use of imagery
2 Uses a relevant quotation but does not explore it
3 Identifies a language feature (simile)
4 An embedded quotation with some comment, but this could be explored more
5 Further comment but the language is too informal

Romeo sees Juliet as beautiful and uses lots of imagery to show this.**1** He says 'she doth teach the torches to burn bright!' (1.5 43)**2** and compares her using a simile**3** to 'a rich jewel' saying that she is worth a great deal.**4** This shows the audience that he thinks she is gorgeous and that he fancies her.**5**

Sample essays

The style of this answer is grade C. There are accurate comments and the answer does not simply retell the story. The reason the candidate stops moving up the mark scheme beyond grade C is that the answer often says things in the simplest way. The points are correct, but in each case more could be said that would show a deeper understanding of how Romeo views Juliet.

The mark scheme for this question **in an examination** would ask the examiner to look out for:
- sustained response to the presentation of Romeo and his feelings for Juliet (AO1)
- effective use of details to support interpretation (AO1)
- explanation of effects of writer's uses of language, structure and form (AO2)
- appropriate comment on themes/ideas and settings (AO2)

These elements are beginning to show here, but this is not sustained yet and there is not enough use of details and examination of language to gain a higher mark.

Question 4 (higher tier: AQA, CCEA exam)

How is the character of Friar Lawrence presented and developed in the play?

Grade-A* answer

Friar Lawrence is presented by Shakespeare as a character around whom much of the action of the play revolves. He is revealed as a man with good intentions, but whose advice has disastrous results on the lives of many of the other characters. By presenting him as a flawed individual, Shakespeare injects realism and believability into the character.

This is a strong opening. There is a clear, bold statement which lets the examiner know exactly what the candidate is going to explore in the rest of the essay. It is obvious from this opening that the candidate recognises the importance of Friar Lawrence's character, and that the character is a construct of Shakespeare's, showing their awareness of form. The examiner would expect the candidate to develop these ideas in the main body of the essay and give detailed references.

The main part of the answer would cover a wide range of comments and explorations of both the character and the themes of the play, making some references to context and perhaps a film version the candidate has seen. An A* answer would tend to give more detailed, exploratory, confident and more developed comment than that at grades C or B.

The essay might progress along these lines:

First, it is notable that Shakespeare has decided to make the character who is Romeo and Juliet's principal confidant and adviser, a man of the church.[1] Even now but even more so at the time the play was written, a priest would be seen as someone fit to advise others on their behaviour; so by doing this, Shakespeare sets the audience up to put some faith, just as Romeo and Juliet do, in his counsel.[2] However, it is clear from his early advice to Romeo and the immediate contradiction that follows, that the Friar is just an ordinary human being as fallible as any other character in the play or otherwise. He tells Romeo off for his fickle nature crying:

'Holy Saint Francis, what a change is here!

Is Rosaline, that thou didst love so dear,

So soon forsaken?...'[3]

This clearly suggests that he doubts the depth of Romeo's feelings[4] and this is reinforced when he states, '...Young men's love then lies/Not truly in their hearts, but in their eyes'.[5] In this metaphor, the Friar goes further in suggesting that Romeo's love is no more than physical infatuation, the result of looks and not of any heartfelt, deep conviction[6] and yet, in almost the next breath, he agrees to marry Romeo to Juliet.[7] When Romeo in his delight at the Friar's agreement wishes to hurry things along as fast as possible the Friar says, 'Wisely and slow. They stumble that run fast',[8] suggesting that he does not want to hurry matters as this would be unwise[9] and yet, he marries them that same afternoon even stating, '...we will make short work'.[10] He is a man of the church and yet he marries two young people immediately, when he has just expressed clear doubts as to whether what is between them is actually 'love' at all.[11] Shakespeare makes the answer to why he does this clear; he hopes that by marrying them he will turn the 'rancour' of their elders 'to pure love'.[12] This is interesting given what we have already heard of the feud and seems not a little naive to say the least.[13]

Sidebar annotations:

[1] An awareness that the character is not real, but a construct of Shakespeare's

[2] The effect of this literary device with regard to characterisation

[3] Use of well-chosen quotation to illustrate point, set out correctly

[4] Effect of quoted text — meaning conveyed to audience

[5] Further quotation, embedded skilfully and correctly set out

[6] Awareness and understanding of metaphor — meaning conveyed to audience

[7] Developing line of argument

[8] More well-chosen and well-integrated quotation

[9] Effect of quote

[10] Another quotation that clearly shows the contradictory nature the candidate has said Shakespeare wishes to convey

[11] More explanation of the point

[12] Another quotation that starts to open up the motives of the Friar and explore the presentation of his character further

[13] Interesting and original personal viewpoint which the student will hopefully go on to justify with further examples

---

You need to conclude your essay with a final point that sums up and really clinches the argument you proposed in your opening paragraph and have been elaborating throughout.

You might begin with…

- Overall, then, I think that Shakespeare…
- Finally, it seems clear that the character of the Friar…
- It could be argued then, that the Friar is presented…
- To conclude, it seems evident that Shakespeare…

Somewhere in your conclusion, if not in this opening line, you need to make sure, as with the rest of your essay, that you flag up the author's name. After all, you are writing about what it is you think they have said, how they've said it and how successful you think they've been in conveying their message. You can't do this without referring to them.

To sum up, Shakespeare has created actions and language for the Friar that display his contradictory and fallible nature to us, largely, I feel to reinforce his point about two human tendencies: to act without fully thinking through the results of our actions, and to lay blame for the consequences of our actions on outside forces.**14** 'Unhappy fortune'**15** exclaims the Friar when told that his letter to Romeo has miscarried; and when he discovers the bodies of Paris and Romeo he cries, 'Ah, what an unkind hour/is guilty of this lamentable chance!'**16** Both statements clearly reveal that he blames what has happened not on his own misguided advice and actions, but on 'fortune' or luck and on time itself, personified here as 'unkind'.**17** Of course, the biggest irony of all with regards to the Friar's character is that he does actually achieve his goal of 'turning' the hatred between the two feuding families 'to pure love' as the play ends with their complete reconciliation, however, not quite in the way he had hoped for! In him, Shakespeare creates an engaging and interesting character, largely because he is fallible and therefore very human, just like the rest of us.**18**

14 Clearly linked to the essay title

15 Well-chosen, brief and embedded quotation

16 More well-chosen quotation, illustrative of concluding point

17 Understanding of personification and its effect — what this conveys to audience

18 A personal, individualised and imaginative response

This is a well-written and observant conclusion. It contains clear statements that go beyond simply summing up events. There is analysis of the Friar's role in the play and an exploration of how Shakespeare has presented and developed (key words in the question) him to make him believable and engaging.

Although not a complete answer — the middle section would need several more points — this entirely fulfils the Assessment Objectives for the top band:

- AO1: insightful exploration of the task, character, themes conveyed through that character and detailed references to the text to support all views offered.
- AO2: evaluation of the writer's uses of language and/or structure and/or form and effects on readers.

Question 5 (Edexcel Controlled Assessment)

Topic: themes

Explore the ways the theme of order and chaos is presented in both the play text and the Luhrmann film version of *Romeo and Juliet*. Support your answer with examples from the text.

1 Quite a lot of narrative detail

2 Relevant quotation

3 Some explanation of the quotation, although this could be explored in more detail.

4 A link to chaos and a brief comment on the rest of the play, which could be more fully developed

5 Film technique correctly identified

6 Technique linked to how chaos is created, but could be developed further

7 Comment on how the action relates to Verona but this needs further development

8 A good final comment on the fire and how it represents chaos, but could be linked to dialogue or another moment from the play

9 Rather too much narrative detail here

10 Correctly laid out quotation

11 Brief comment on the quotation but this could be developed

12 A little more comment on the quotation and why the chaos has occurred

13 More narrative detail

14 Reasonable focus on the presentation of the Prince as a figure of authority in the film

15 A good contrast between the two moments in the scene is made here

16 A good comment on the structure of the play overall. This needs more development

Grade-C essay

There is a lot of chaos in the play 'Romeo and Juliet'. At the start of the play there is a big fight in the street where the servants of the two families argue with each other.**1** Sampson and Gregory insult the Montagues by saying: 'A dog of the house of Montague moves me.' (line 7)**2** which is insulting to them.**3** When they bite their thumbs at them this provokes them into a fight. It is this chaotic behaviour that causes a lot of the problems later on in the play.**4**

This opening reflects the demands of the question and makes it clear that the response will focus on order and chaos and how they are presented in the play. Again, there is no list of events, which is a good approach.

This is also shown clearly in the film with lots of action and sudden movement in the opening scene. The director uses lots of quick shots,**5** cutting from one person to another rapidly to show the chaotic nature of the scene.**6** One of the servants is continually bashed over the head with a woman's handbag, showing how their riots are affecting everyone else in Verona.**7** The scene ends with a huge fire at the petrol station where it has been set in a more modern manner. The fire is a way of representing chaos in a dramatic and interesting visual way.**8**

The candidate now links the play with the film version. Words such as 'also' are good linking words.

The Prince has to stop the fight and he tells them to throw their weapons to the ground before giving us some background information on what has been happening:**9**

'Three civil brawls, bred of an airy word

By thee, old Capulet, and Montague,

Have thrice disturbed the quiet of our streets'**10**

Which shows that there has been chaos for some time.**11** It seems the only reason the fights are occurring is because of 'an airy word' which does not seem a good enough reason for a fight.**12** He tells them that if it happens once more they will be executed: 'Your lives shall pay the forfeit of the peace' (line 88).**13** The film presents the Prince as angry, but he is dressed impressively as a Chief of Police, to show his authority and his ability to re-establish order in the streets.**14** The scene is much quieter than the first scene to emphasise the calm nature of the meeting with Capulet and Montague, apart from the Prince's anger.**15** This is like a lot of scenes in the play where there has been a moment of dramatic chaotic action followed by the calm of the aftermath.**16**

90   PHILIP ALLAN LITERATURE GUIDE FOR GCSE

Sample essays

The style of this answer is grade C. There are accurate comments and the answer does not simply retell the story. The reason the candidate stops moving up the mark scheme beyond grade C is that the answer often says things in the simplest way. The points are correct, but in each case more could be said that would show a deeper understanding. The elements of a higher grade answer are beginning to show here, but this is not sustained yet and there is not enough reference to detail and examination of language used to gain a higher mark.

Review your learning

(Answers are given on p. 94.)

1. What is the best way to use a quotation?
2. What should you say in your essay about the purpose of a text?
3. What are the key features of a good literature essay?
4. How easy is it to move up through the grades?

More interactive questions and answers online.

Answers

Context (p. 11)

1 Context means the factors influencing the play when it was written and set. These factors could include attitudes to the way people lived, what they did for a living, their leisure activities, religious beliefs, attitudes to women, sex, marriage, money, moral issues, issues of class, the monarchy, race, and any other issues that were specific to this period (1595). All of these things will have influenced what Shakespeare has written and how his audiences, then and since, have responded to his plays.

2 Many elements of the play are typical of the time, such as the masque in Act 1 scene 5, the issue of arranged marriages and feuds between families. Duelling was fashionable then, but is not now. Some issues raised by the play can still be said to be relevant today, e.g. the question of what being in love is really based upon (looks or character and values), and the question of who we blame when things go wrong.

3 This is two-fold. First, people were becoming interested in travel abroad and so many would come to watch the play to see something about foreign customs. Second, Shakespeare had to be sure not to offend his patroness Queen Elizabeth I by appearing critical or questioning of any of the values and belief systems of the English society that she ruled; setting the play in Italy gave him licence to raise as many questions he wanted as he could simply say that he was writing about Italy.

Plot and structure (p. 31)

1 Any ten can be selected as long as you back up your point, but these may include:
- the fight scene in Act 1 scene 1
- Romeo and Juliet's first meeting
- the balcony scene
- the wedding
- Capulet forcing Juliet to marry Paris
- Romeo killing Tybalt
- Tybalt killing Mercutio
- the letter not getting to Romeo
- the Prince banishing Romeo
- the death of Romeo
- the death of Juliet

Answers

2 Tybalt has a violent side to his character, which he uses to provoke violence in others. He says Benvolio is hypocritical for asking him to put his sword away when he has drawn his own sword.
   Benvolio tries to keep things calm when there is a threat to peace.
3 The relationship of the two lovers highlights how haste can cause problems, but it also highlights the problems of the feud and the problems of arranged marriages.
4 The ending sees an end to the feud and the families reconciled, so the play progresses from violence at the start to peace and harmony at the end.

Characterisation (p. 45)

1 See the *Characterisation* section for detailed references about each of the major characters and for quotations that help to define them.
2 See p. 32.
3 See p. 34.
4 Romeo changes very little as he is highly emotional, impetuous, passionate and rash in his actions throughout the play.
   Juliet changes the most, from living in a state of innocence to becoming deceitful as a means of remaining true to her own values.
   Friar Lawrence changes from believing he can sort out the problems of the two families to realising that he has merely meddled and with disastrous results, though he never fully accepts the degree to which he is to blame.
   The Nurse changes very little, although Juliet loses her faith in the trustworthiness of the Nurse during the play.
5 a Romeo and Juliet — passionate love, perhaps based on physical attraction only.
   b The Capulets and the Montagues — deep hatred and a feud.
   c Juliet and the Nurse are close until the Nurse suggests that Juliet may as well marry Paris even though she is already married to Romeo.
   d Romeo and Friar Lawrence — trust; the Friar is almost a father figure to Romeo.
   e Romeo and Tybalt — Tybalt hates Romeo, but Romeo only wants to kill Tybalt after Mercutio has been murdered.

Style (p. 57)

1 Prose: Sampson, Gregory, the other servants, the Nurse. They are the lower characters, but note that Mercutio speaks in prose at times, perhaps illustrative of his disjointed or agitated state of mind.

Poetry: Romeo, Juliet, Friar Lawrence, Capulet and all of the other noble characters who are higher in status.
2 Examples can be found on p. 51.
3 Examples can be found on p. 52.

Themes (p. 63)

1 Look back at the sub-headings of this chapter.
2 Other themes might include: parenting; the role of the church in our lives; the danger of an exaggerated sense of honour; the destructiveness of male pride; the dangers of an over-oppressive upbringing for women.
3 Romeo and Juliet, the Friar, Lady and Lord Capulet.
4 Romeo and Juliet, the Friar, Mercutio, Lords Montague and Capulet.
5 All of them.

Tackling the assessments (p. 75)

1 The word 'essay' means 'an attempt' and is usually one person's thoughts on a given subject. You will find yourself attempting to put across your thoughts on a particular area of the play when you write in the examination.
2 See 'Planning your answer' on p. 66.
3 See 'Using PEE effectively' on p. 69.
4 See 'Getting an A*' on p. 75.

Assessment Objectives and skills (p. 80)

1–4 See pp. 76–79.
5 If you don't know, ask your teacher. See p. 76.
6 Do not: retell the story, quote long passages, merely identify figures of speech or other features with no explanation of effect, give unsubstantiated opinions.

Sample essays (p. 91)

1 See 'Using quotations and referring to the text' on p. 84.
2 If the question allows it you should always try to say something about the writer's purpose. This shows that you appreciate that the play is fiction (not real) and that you understand that the writer set out to achieve something specific.
3 See 'Structuring your essay' on p. 81.
4 Always aim high. Don't model your writing on a grade-C answer when you can model it on a grade-A* answer. Look carefully at what these examples teach you and develop these skills through practice.